Chic
&Easy
Beading

Vol.3

KALMBACH BOOKS

Kalmbach Books
21027 Crossroads Circle
Waukesha, Wisconsin 53186
www.kalmbach.com/books

Published in 2009
13 12 11 10 09 1 2 3 4 5

Manufactured in the United States of America

ISBN: 978-0-87116-277-9

The material in this book has appeared previously in *Bead&Button* magazine. *Bead&Button* is registered as a trademark.

Publisher's Cataloging-in-Publication Data

Chic & easy beading.

     v. : col. ill. ; cm.

     "Bead & button books."
   Vol. 1 edited by Alice Korach ; Vol. 2 edited by Julia Gelach, Cheryl Phelan, Lesley Weiss.
     ISBN: 0-89024-438-3 (v. 1)
     ISBN: 0-87116-225-3 (v. 2)
     ISBN: 978-087116-277-9 (v. 3)

1. Beadwork--Handbooks, manuals, etc. 2. Beadwork--Patterns. 3. Jewelry making--Handbooks, manuals, etc. I. Korach, Alice. II. Gerlach, Julia R. III. Phelan, Cheryl. IV. Weiss, Lesley. V. Kalmbach Publishing Company. VI. Title: Chic and easy beading

TT860 .C48 2004
745.594/2

Introduction

In an increasingly fast-paced world, beginning and accomplished beaders alike need quick and easy projects that will still look good and highlight their stylish sensibilities. *Chic&Easy Beading, Vol. 3*, provides those projects, showcasing jewelry pieces created using stringing, wirework, and the simplest beadweaving techniques.

The first two volumes of *Chic&Easy* were collected from the three *Chic&Easy* special issues, as well as the pages of *Bead&Button* magazine. This third volume brings you more of what made those book great — a collection of stylish jewelry projects from *Bead&Button* that requires only basic skills and a small amount of free time. All the projects have been fully tested by the editors, and comprehensive Basics and Tools & Materials sections ensure that beaders of all levels will

be ready to make the necklaces, bracelets, and earrings included in these pages.

From crystals to gemstones, metal and chain to pearls and shells, *Chic&Easy* is loaded with different materials, styles, and beading techniques. Want to try your hand at some simple wirework? Charlotte Miller's imaginative "Upside down" earrings (p. 112) will be a perfect fit. Want to display some big, beautiful gemstones or delicate lampworked beads? Try Nancy Sells Puffer's "Lampwork and gemstones" necklace (below right and p. 12) on for size. Or do you just like the look of pearls draped around your wrist? The bracelet from Maryann Scandiffio-Humes's "Pearls just want to have fun" (below left and p. 128)

offers dancing pearl dangles. Many materials for these projects can be found at your local bead or craft store. Other places to look for hard-to-find supplies are given in the Materials lists.

Turn the page for 56 wireworking, basic bead stitching, and stringing projects, each piece chic and easy to make.

Tools & Materials
Essential supplies for making beautiful jewelry

TOOLS

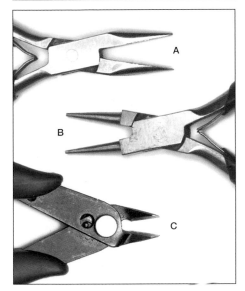

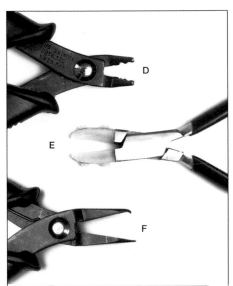

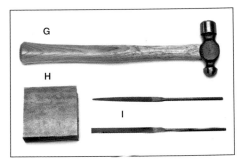

Chainnose pliers (A) have smooth, flat inner jaws, and the tips taper to a point. Use them for gripping and for opening and closing loops and jump rings.
Roundnose pliers (B) have smooth, tapered, conical jaws used to make loops. The closer to the tip you work, the smaller the loop will be.
With diagonal wire cutters (C), use the front of the blades to make a pointed cut and the back of the blades to make a flat cut.

Crimping pliers (D) have two grooves in their jaws that are used to fold or roll a crimp bead into a compact shape.
Nylon-jaw pliers (E) feature a replaceable nylon lining on each jaw that protect wire from marking. They are also useful for straightening wire.
Use split-ring pliers (F) to simplify opening split rings by inserting a curved jaw between the wires.

A hammer (G) is used to harden wire for hoops and bangles. Any hammer with a flat head will work, as long as the head is free of nicks that could mar your metal. The light ball-peen hammer shown here is one of the most commonly used hammers for jewelry making.
A bench block (H) provides a hard, smooth surface on which to hammer your pieces. An anvil is similarly hard but has different surfaces, such as a tapered horn, to help forge wire into different shapes.
Metal files (I) are used to refine and shape the edges of metal and wire surfaces.

Bentnose pliers have a slight bend near the tip, making them easier to use in some jewelry making.

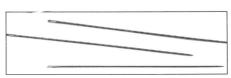

Beading needles are coded by size. The higher the number, the finer the beading needle. Unlike sewing needles, the eye of a beading needle is almost as narrow as its shaft. The size of the bead and the number of times you will pass the needle through the bead affect the needle size that you will use — if you pass through a bead multiple times, you need to use a smaller needle.

Design boards have grooves in them for strands of beads, helping you see what the necklace will look like when assembled.

FINDINGS

A **head pin** looks like a blunt, long, thick sewing pin. It has a flat or decorative head on one end to keep beads on. Head pins come in different diameters (or gauges) and lengths.

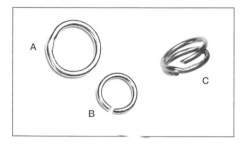

A **jump ring** is used to connect two components. It is a small wire circle or oval that is either soldered (**A**) or comes with an opening (**B**).

Split rings (C) are used like jump rings but are much more secure. They look like tiny key rings and are made of springy wire.

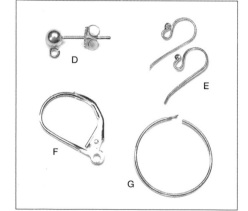

Earring findings come in a huge variety of metals and styles, including **post (D)**, **French hook (E)**, **lever-back (F)**, and **hoop (G)**. You will almost always want a loop (or loops) on earring findings so you can attach beads.

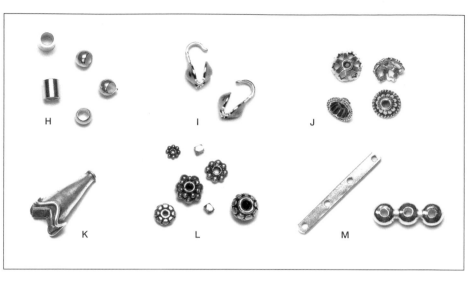

Crimp beads (H) are small, large-holed, thin-walled metal beads designed to be flattened or crimped into a tight roll. Use them when stringing jewelry on flexible beading wire.

Bead tips (I) are small metal beads primarily used to link a strand of beads on a cord to a clasp. They come in a clamshell or basket shape. Clamshell bead tips close over a knot to hide it. The knot rests against the basket in basket-shaped bead tips.

Bead caps (J) are used to decorate a bead or gemstone.

Cones (K) have openings at both ends, one large and one small. They are ideal for concealing the knotted ends of a tassel or multistrand necklace.

Spacers (L) are small beads used between larger beads to space the placement of the beads.

Spacer bars (M) are used to hold multiple strands of a necklace in alignment so it drapes well. They are usually inserted at intervals while stringing the beads, and also help prevent tangling.

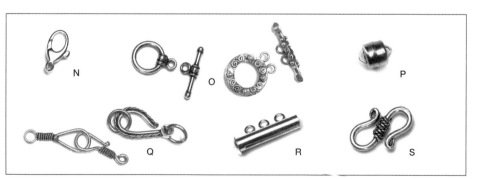

Clasps come in many sizes and shapes. Some of the most common are the **lobster claw (N)**, which opens when you pull a tiny lever; the **toggle (O)**, consisting of a ring and a bar; the **magnetic barrel (P)**, two pieces held together with a magnet; the **hook-and-eye (Q)**, consisting of a hook and a jump ring or split ring; **the slide (R)**, consisting of one tube that slides inside another; and the **S-hook (S)**, which links two soldered jump rings or split rings.

STRINGING MATERIALS

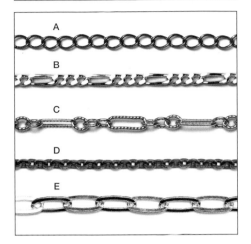

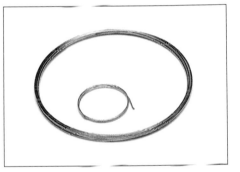

Chain is available in many finishes, including sterling silver and gold-filled as well as base metal or plated metals, and styles, including **curb (A)**, **figaro (B)**, **long-and-short (C)**, **rolo (D)**, and **cable (E)**.

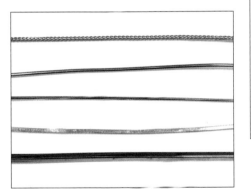

Wire is available in a number of materials and finishes, including brass, gold, gold-filled, gold-plated, fine silver, sterling silver, anodized niobium (chemically colored wire), and copper. Brass, copper, and craft wire are packaged in 10–40-yd. (9.5–36.6m) spools, while gold, silver, and niobium are usually sold by the foot or ounce. Wire thickness is measured by gauge — the higher the gauge, the thinner the wire — and is available in varying hardnesses and shapes, including twisted, round, half-round, and square.

Flexible beading wire is composed of steel wires twisted together and covered with nylon. This wire is much stronger than thread and does not stretch; the higher the number of inner strands (between three and 49), the more flexible and kink-resistant the wire. It is available in a variety of sizes. Use .014 and .015 for most gemstones, crystals, and glass beads. Use thicker varieties, .018, .019, and .024, for heavy beads or nuggets. Use thinner wire, .010 and .012, for lightweight pieces and beads with very small holes, such as pearls.

Memory wire is steel spring wire. It comes in several sizes and can be used without clasps to make coiled bracelets, necklaces, and rings.

Fibers offer another option for stringing. Leather and suede can be colorful or earthy. Waxed cotton and linen cords are stronger than leather or suede, so they are also good choices. Ribbons and yarns come in many colors and styles, from very thin to extra wide. You can either tie the ends of the fiber together or attach a **crimp end (F)** or **pinch end cap (G)** to finish.

Basics

WIREWORK
Cutting beading wire

Most instructions recommend a wire length. If none is given (or to adjust the given length), decide how long your necklace will be, add 6 in. (15cm) (5 in./13cm for a bracelet), and cut a piece of beading wire to that length.

Cutting memory wire

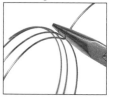

Memory wire is hardened steel, so it will dent and ruin the jaws of most wire cutters. Use heavy-duty wire cutters or cutters specifically designed for memory wire, or bend the wire back and forth until it snaps.

Loops, plain

1 Using chainnose pliers, make a right-angle bend approximately ¼ in. (6mm) from the end of the wire.
2 Grip the tip of the wire with roundnose pliers. Press downward slightly, and rotate the wire into a loop.
3 Let go, then grip the loop at the same place on the pliers, and keep turning to close the loop.
4 The closer to the tip of the roundnose pliers that you work, the smaller the loop will be.

Loops, wrapped

1 Using chainnose pliers, make a right-angle bend approximately 1¼ in. (3.2cm) from the end of the wire.
2 Position the jaws of your roundnose pliers in the bend.
3 Curve the short end of the wire over the top jaw of the roundnose pliers.
4 Reposition the pliers so the lower jaw fits snugly in the loop. Curve the wire downward around the bottom jaw of the pliers. This is the first half of a wrapped loop.
5 To complete the wraps, grasp the top of the loop with chainnose pliers.
6 Wrap the wire around the stem two or three times. Trim the excess wire, and gently press the cut end close to the wraps with chainnose pliers.

Making a set of wraps above a top-drilled bead

1 Center a top-drilled bead on a 3-in. (7.6cm) piece of wire. Bend each wire end upward, crossing them into an X above the bead.
2 Using chainnose pliers, make a small bend in each wire end so they form a right angle.
3 Wrap the horizontal wire around the vertical wire as in a wrapped loop. Trim the excess wrapping wire. If you need to add a loop, make it with the vertical wire, directly above these wraps.

Crimping

1 Position the crimp bead in the hole of the crimping pliers that is closest to the handle.
2 Holding the wires apart, squeeze the tool to compress the crimp bead, making sure one wire is on each side of the dent.
3 Place the crimp bead in the front hole of the tool, and position it so the dent is facing outward. Squeeze the tool to fold the crimp in half.

Tug on the wires to ensure that the crimp is secure.

Folded crimp

1 Hold the crimp using the tip of your chainnose pliers. Squeeze the pliers firmly to flatten the crimp.

2 Tug the wire to make sure the crimp is secure. If the wire slides, repeat the steps with a new crimp.

Opening and closing plain loops and jump rings

1 Hold a loop or jump ring with two pairs of chainnose pliers or with chain-nose and bentnose pliers.

2 To open the loop or jump ring, bring the tips of one pair of pliers toward you and push the tips of the other pair away.

3 Reverse the steps to close the loop or jump ring.

Opening split rings

Slide the hooked tip of split-ring pliers between the two overlapping wires.

THREAD
Stop bead

Use a stop bead to secure beads temporarily when you begin stitching. Choose a bead that is distinctly different from the beads in your project. String the stop bead about 6 in. (15cm) from the end of your thread, and go back through it in the same direction. If desired, go through it one more time for added security.

Conditioning thread

Use either beeswax (not candle wax or paraffin) or Thread Heaven to condition nylon thread (Nymo). Beeswax smooths the nylon fibers and adds tackiness that will stiffen your beadwork slightly. Thread Heaven adds a static charge that causes the thread to repel itself, so don't use it with doubled thread. Stretch the thread, then pull it through the conditioner, starting with the end that comes off the spool first.

KNOTTING
Overhand knot

Make a loop at the end of the thread. Pull the short tail through the loop, and tighten.

Lark's head knot

Fold a cord in half and lay it behind a ring, loop, bar, etc. with the fold pointing down. Bring the ends through the ring from back to front, then through the fold and tighten.

Square knot

Cross the left-hand end of the thread over the right, and bring it around and back up. Cross the end that is now on the right over the left, go through the loop, and pull both ends to tighten.

Half-hitch knot

Pass the needle under the thread between two beads. A loop will form as you pull the thread through. Cross over the thread between the beads, sew through the loop, and pull gently to draw the knot into the beadwork.

Surgeon's knot

Cross the left-hand end of the thread over and under the right twice. Pull the ends to tighten. Cross the end that is now on the right over the left, go through the loop, and tighten.

CHAPTER 1

necklaces

Lampwork and gemstones

Stone nuggets partner with lampworked beads in this classic necklace. Silver tube beads curve around the larger beads in a second strand that accents the colors of the lampworked pieces.

designed by **Nancy Sells Puffer**

MATERIALS

necklace 19 in. (48cm)
- Hill Tribes silver pendant
- 4 25 x 20mm (approx.) flat gemstone nuggets
- 6 23 x 15mm (approx.) gemstone nuggets
- 9 11 x 17mm lampworked beads
- 22 5mm silver beads
- 2–3g 3.8mm silver tube beads (Fire Mountain Gems, firemountaingems.com)
- 4–6 size 8º seed beads
- 18 8mm flat silver spacers
- 13mm lobster claw clasp
- 1 in. (2.5cm) chain, 6mm links
- 2-in. (5cm) head pin
- 2 crimp beads
- flexible beading wire, .019
- chainnose pliers
- clamps or tape
- crimping pliers
- roundnose pliers
- wire cutters

step*by*step

[1] Determine the finished length of your necklace (this one is 19 in./48cm), add 4 in. (10cm), and cut a piece of beading wire (Basics, p. 8) to that length. Cut a second piece of flexible beading wire 6 in. (15cm) longer than the first.

[2] Clamp or tape one end of the shorter wire, and center the pendant on it. To fill the pendant's bail, string one or more 8º seed beads, so subsequent beads will stay past the bail's edges **(photo a)**.

[3] String a 5mm silver bead, a 23 x 15mm nugget, a 5mm, a spacer, a lampworked bead, a spacer, a 5mm, a 25 x 20mm flat nugget, a 5mm, a spacer, a lampworked bead, and a spacer **(photo b)**. Repeat.

[4] String a 5mm and a 23 x 15mm nugget. Secure the end of the wire with a clamp or tape **(photo c)**.

[5] Remove the clamp or tape from the other wire end. Repeat steps 3 and 4.

[6] To attach the second wire, remove the clamp or tape from one end of the beaded wire, and hold the ends of the two wires together. Over both ends, string two 5mms, a crimp bead, and the end chain link (to create an extender chain). Go back through the beads just strung **(photo d)**. Tighten the wires, and crimp the crimp bead (Basics). Trim the excess wire.

[7] On the second wire, string approximately 3 in. (7.6cm) of silver tube beads. Skip the next few beads, and go through the second lampworked bead from the end and the spacers surrounding it **(photo e)**. Make sure the strand of tube beads is long enough to arc gracefully over the larger beads. Repeat, going through the fourth lampworked bead and the spacers surrounding it.

[8] String approximately 1½ in. (3.8cm) of tube beads, and go through the pendant's loop. String the tube beads on the second half of the necklace to match the first.

[9] To attach the clasp, repeat step 6, substituting a lobster claw clasp for the chain.

[10] To add a dangle to the extender chain, string a spacer, a lampworked bead, and a spacer on the head pin. Make the first half of a wrapped loop (Basics), attach the end chain link, and finish the wraps. Trim the excess wire.

SUPPLY NOTE:
Nancy created the lampworked beads featured here. Contact her at nancysellsglass.com.

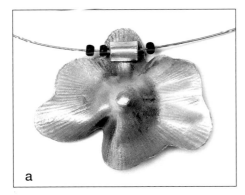

a

b

c

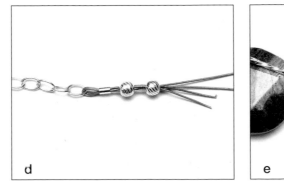

d

e

Leaf necklace

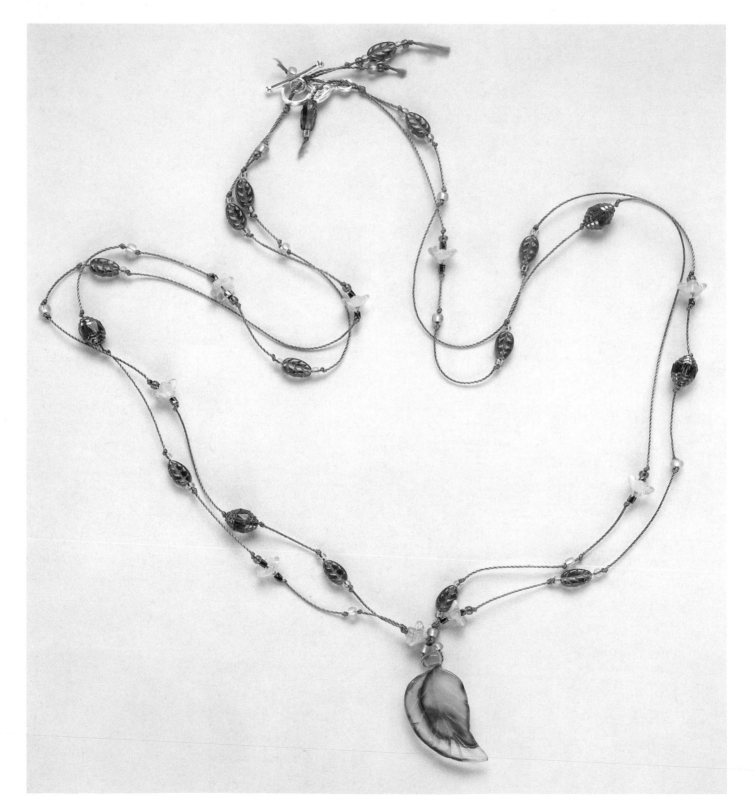

This simple two-strand leaf necklace is a perfect example of "less is more." It's a great accessory for an outfit that doesn't want to play second fiddle to a major necklace. It's also a good way to use a medium or large focal bead without the density of a full string of support beads or the time commitment of multiple strands.

MATERIALS
necklace 20 in. (51cm)
- 24 x 16mm agate leaf pendant
- 4 8mm amber glass beads
- 13 6–8mm pressed-glass leaves
- 9 6mm pressed-glass flower beads
- 2g 8º seed beads in assorted colors
- toggle clasp
- 8 ft. (2.5m) nylon beading cord, size 1–3
- awl

by **Debbie Nishihara**

step*by*step

[1] Cut two 48-in. (1.2m) lengths of cord. On one cord, center an 8º seed bead, the leaf pendant, and an 8º. Over both ends of the cord, string an 8º and tie an overhand knot (Basics, p. 8, and photo a) above the seed beads, leaving a little slack. These two strands will make up one side of the necklace.
[2] String a flower bead over both ends of the second cord. Pull the bead down to form a loop at the center of the cord (photo b).
[3] Place the loop behind the space between the 8ºs on the other cord. There

should be two 8ºs two below it and one 8º above (photo c). Pass the ends and flower bead through the loop, forming a lark's head knot (Basics and photo d), and pull the knot tight so the flower bead is flush against the space between the 8ºs (photo e). String an 8º next to the flower bead, and tie an overhand knot snug against the 8º. These new cords make up the remaining side of the necklace.
[4] Randomly string the 8ºs, leaves, flowers, and glass beads one strand at a time, tying an overhand knot below and above each bead or group of beads. Use an awl to position the knots against the beads (photo f).

[5] After adding the accent beads, hold up the necklace and decide where you want the clasp. Knot the two strands of one side together with an overhand knot, string on half of a clasp on one of the strands, and tie the two strands together again with another overhand knot (photo g).
[6] Repeat on the other side. String a few beads on each cord end and secure with an overhand knot. Trim off the ends, and fray the remaining bit of cord after the knot by twisting it back and forth between your fingers (photo h).

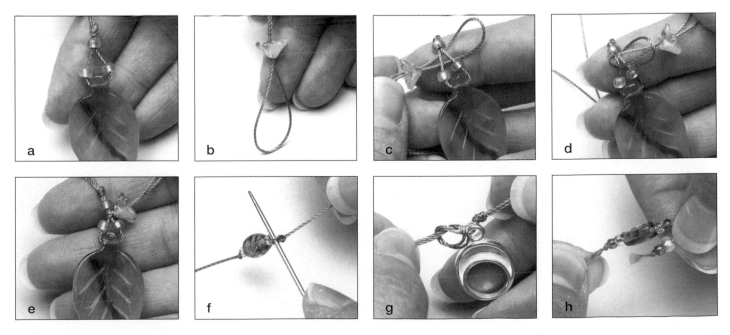

a
b
c
d
e
f
g
h

Seed bead serpentine

Add textural interest to a double-strand necklace by winding seed beads along a natural path to a lampworked focal bead.

designed by **Dale Feuer**

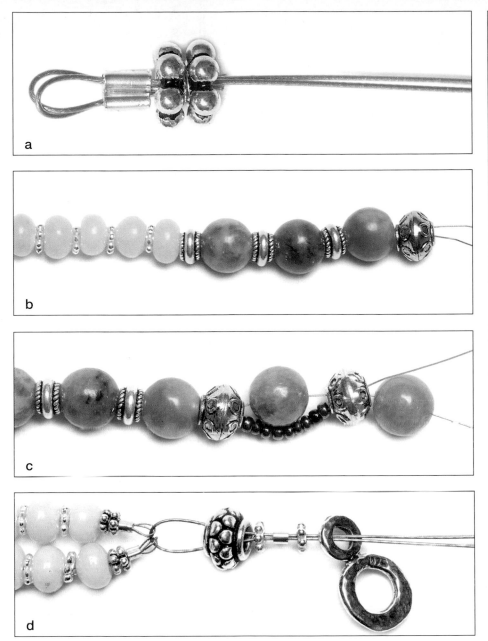

a

b

c

d

MATERIALS

necklace 18 in. (46cm)

- 25–45mm lampworked focal bead
- 70–80 5–9mm gemstone or glass
  beads, in 2 or 3 colors
- 1g size 11º seed beads in
  various colors
- 2 spacers with 5mm holes
- 72–80 4–5mm spacers
- clasp
- 6 crimp beads
- flexible beading wire, .010 and .014
- clamps or tape
- crimping pliers
- wire cutters

String the second side to mirror the first side of the strand. Clamp or tape the strand.

[7] Repeat steps 1–6 to make a second two-wire strand, but omit one bead and spacer on each side of the focal bead. Pass both wires through the focal bead and the adjacent spacers, and complete the second side.

[8] Snug up the beads on both strands, remove the clamps or tape, and finish the ends the same that way you started them in step 1, positioning the spacer and crimp bead close to the last bead before making the loop.

Clasp

[1] Cut a 10-in. (25cm) piece of .014 beading wire. On one side of the necklace, center the wire loops on the 10-in. (25cm) wire.

[2] Over both ends, string a 5mm-hole spacer, a 4–5mm spacer, a crimp bead, a 4–5mm spacer, and half of a clasp (photo d). Go back through the beads just strung.

[3] Tighten the beading wire so the 5mm-hole spacer covers the crimp beads on the strands. Crimp the crimp bead, and trim the tails. Repeat on the other end.

step*by*step

Necklace

Decide on the stringing pattern for both strands of your necklace. Plan two patterns of alternating 5–9mm beads and 4–5mm spacers for each strand (section A and section B). This necklace has a 5-in. (13cm) pattern A and a 3-in. (7.6cm) pattern B. Pattern B is embellished with seed beads.

[1] Cut two 30-in. (76cm) pieces of .010 beading wire (Basics, p. 8). With the wire ends flush on one end, string a spacer and a crimp bead over both wires. Go back through the crimp bead and the spacer, leaving an ⅛-in. (3mm) loop. Crimp the crimp bead (Basics), and trim the tails close to the spacer (photo a).

[2] Over both wires, string the pattern A beads, ending with a spacer (photo b).

[3] Separate the wires. On one wire, begin pattern B. String a 5–9mm bead and a spacer.

[4] On the other wire, string enough seed beads to fit alongside the 5–9mm bead, and go through the spacer (photo c).

[5] Repeat steps 3 and 4 with the remaining pattern B beads, alternating whether the seed beads are positioned to the left or right of the 5–9mms.

[6] Over both wires, string a spacer, a focal bead, and a spacer.

Chain and simple

Instant-gratification projects are a must in any beader's repertoire. Whether you need a quick beading fix or want to make an elegant necklace fast, this project is for you.

designed by **Gloria Farver**

a

b

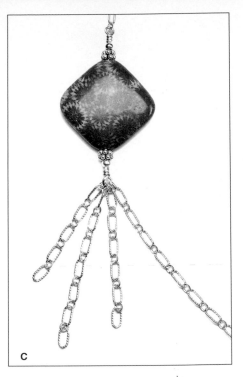

c

d

EDITOR'S NOTE:
Chain in a wide variety of styles has become readily available in the past few years. If you can't find the specific chain used here, try a different style that complements your stones. Here, faceted rhodonite is paired with elongated curb chain.

step*by*step

[1] Cut chain to the following lengths, leaving a short link on each end:
• one 23½-in. (59.7cm) piece
• one 7¾-in. (19.7cm) piece
• two 6⅝-in. (16.8cm) pieces
  Cut chain to the following lengths, leaving a short link on one end and a long link on the other end:
• two 2⅜-in. (6cm) pieces
• two 2-in. (5cm) pieces
• two 1¾-in. (4.4cm) pieces

[2] Cut two 4-in. (10cm) pieces of wire.

[3] Make the first half of a wrapped loop (Basics, p. 8) at one end of a wire, and attach it to an end link of a 6⅝-in. chain. Finish the wraps **(photo a)**.

[4] On the wire, string a 2mm saucer bead, two 5mm flat spacers, a gemstone bead, two 5mms, and a 2mm. Make the first half of a wrapped loop **(photo b)**.

[5] On the wrapped loop, string the 7¾-in. chain and the short-link end of one of each pair of the three short chains. Finish the wraps **(photo c)**.

[6] Repeat steps 3–5 with the remaining short chains and the remaining end link of the 7¾-in. chain.

[7] Open a jump ring (Basics), and attach it to half of a clasp, an end link of the 23½-in. chain, and an end link of

MATERIALS
necklace 24 in. (61cm)
• 2 1 x ⅝-in. (25 x 16mm) gemstone beads
• 4 2mm saucer beads
• 8 5mm flat spacers
• clasp
• 8 in. (20cm) 20-gauge wire, half-hard
• 5 ft. (1.5m) long-and-short cable chain, 6mm and 3mm links
• 2 4mm jump rings
• chainnose pliers
• roundnose pliers
• wire cutters

the beaded chain **(photo d)**. Close the jump ring. Repeat with the other half of the clasp.

Neckline variations

Because this design includes both scoop- and V-neck lines, this necklace looks terrific with many wardrobe choices. Charlotte seed beads with a cut on one side add extra sparkle.

designed by **Gloria Farver**

a

b

c

MATERIALS

necklace 22 in. (56cm)

- 10 x 5mm faceted crystal teardrop
- 2 6mm accent beads
- 16-in. (41cm) strand 4 x 5mm faceted rondelles
- hank Charlotte seed beads, size 13º
- 13mm vermeil flower cone (Tiger Tiger, tiger-tiger.com)
- 10 4mm spacers
- clasp
- 4 crimp beads
- flexible beading wire, .010
- clamps or tape
- crimping pliers
- wire cutters

d

e

EDITOR'S NOTE:

When using size .010 flexible beading wire, always check to make sure that the inside of each crimp bead is smooth and perfect. Crimp firmly, because this fine wire cuts and slips easily.

step*by*step

[1] Cut one 30-in. (76cm) and one 23-in. (58cm) piece of flexible beading wire (Basics, p. 8).

[2] Center the faceted teardrop on the 30-in. wire, and string both ends through the flower cone (photo a).

[3] String a repeating pattern of six Charlottes and an accent bead twice over both wires. String six more Charlottes (photo b).

[4] Separate the wires, and string a repeating pattern of six Charlottes and a rondelle on each until each side has 3 in. (7.6cm) of beads above the split. End with six Charlottes (photo c). Clamp or tape the wire ends, and set this section aside.

[5] On the 23-in. wire, string nine repeats of six Charlottes and a rondelle. String six more Charlottes and center the beads on the wire.

[6] Remove the clamp or tape from one end of the 30-in. wire, and align it with an end of the short wire. String a faceted rondelle over both wire ends (photo d). String the same alternating pattern of Charlottes and rondelles for about 6 in. (15cm), about 19 repeats.

[7] Over both wires, string two spacer beads, a crimp bead, two spacers, a crimp, a spacer, and half a clasp. Pass the wire ends back through the spacers and crimps. Crimp the crimp beads (photo e and Basics) and trim the excess wire.

[8] Repeat steps 6–7 on the other side. Be sure to snug up all the beads before crimping the second side.

Great lengths

Make a luxurious scarf necklace with long, flowing strands of seed beads. String a second necklace in coordinating colors and enjoy the flexibility of jewelry with interchangeable sections.

designed by **Linda Arline Hartung**

EDITOR'S NOTE:
The beads shown here are Italian seed beads, available through Alacarte Clasps. You can substitute Czech seed beads in size 13° or smaller for these diminutive beauties.

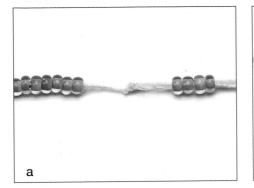

a

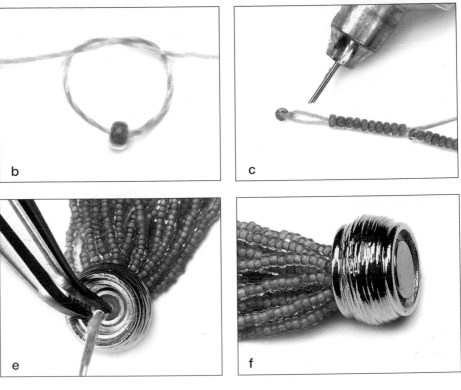

b

c

d

e

f

step*by*step

[1] Cut 40 24 in. (61cm) pieces of nylon beading cord.

[2] Separate one strand of seed beads from its hank. Clamp or tape one end to secure the beads. Tie the other end to a piece of beading cord using a square knot (Basics, p. 8). Slide a few beads off the original strand, over the knot, and onto the cord **(photo a)**. Transfer the rest of the beads from the strand to the cord.

[3] Slide the last bead about 1 in. (2.5cm) away from the rest, and make a square knot over it **(photo b)**.

[4] Place the tail against the 1 in. of exposed cord. Slide eight beads over the tail, positioning them about ¼ in. (6mm) from the knotted bead. To secure the beads, dab the exposed cords with G-S Hypo Cement **(photo c)**, then slide the next eight beads against the knotted bead. Trim the tail. Push all the remaining beads flush against the others at the knot.

[5] Repeat steps 2–4, making a total of 20 beaded cords.

[6] Remove the clamps or tape from the cords. Gather the 20 cords, and glue the ends together using Bond 527 Cement. When the glue is dry, trim the tip of the glued section at an angle with diagonal wire cutters.

[7] String half a clasp over the glued cords **(photo d)**. If needed, use a bead reamer to enlarge the clasp's hole.

[8] String a crimp bead over the glued cords. Pull each cord so the beads are inside the clasp. Dab the cords at the bottom of the clasp with Bond 527 Cement, then push the crimp against the cords while still wet. Flatten the crimp bead (Basics) using bentnose pliers **(photo e)**. Allow the adhesive to dry, then cut the cords close to the crimp.

[9] Repeat steps 2–8 to make the second half of the necklace with seed beads of a different color.

[10] Lightly file the dimpled sides of the two clasp magnets. Place them dimpled-side down into the clasps **(photo f)**. Test the fit by putting the two clasps together, making sure there are no gaps. If the clasp halves are not flush, trim the string closer to the crimp bead, then retest the fit.

[11] Remove the magnets. Mix a small batch of two-part epoxy according to the manufacturer's instructions. With a toothpick, place a liberal amount of glue in a clasp cavity. The glue should overflow slightly.

[12] Press a magnet into the clasp half, dimpled-side down. Apply pressure. Wipe off the excess glue, then apply pressure until the glue sets. Remove any glue residue by wiping the clasp and magnet with a cloth slightly dampened with rubbing alcohol. Repeat with the second magnet and clasp.

MATERIALS
necklace 38½ in. (98cm)

- 2 hanks (24 strands each, 20 in./51cm long) seed beads, size 13⁹ or smaller in coordinating colors
- magnetic barrel clasp* with dimpled magnets (Alacarte Clasps, alacarteclasps.com)
- 2 3 x 2mm crimp beads (2mm hole)
- nylon beading cord, 1/0x
- Bond 527 Cement
- G-S Hypo Cement
- rubbing alcohol (optional)
- toothpick
- two-part epoxy
- bead reamer (optional)
- bentnose pliers
- file or emery board
- wire cutters
- * Note: Pregnant women and people with pacemakers should consult a physician before wearing magnetic jewelry.

Dew drops

With a little ingenuity, you can turn sparkling teardrops and bicone crystals into interesting components on an elegant chain necklace.

by **Anna Elizabeth Draeger**

a

b

step*by*step

[1] String a 4mm bicone crystal on a head pin, and make a plain loop (Basics, p. 8, and **photo a)**. Make a total of 12 short dangles.
[2] Make a long dangle by stringing a bicone, a 6mm rondelle, and a bicone on a head pin. Make a plain loop above the last bicone **(photo b)**.
[3] Cut a 2-in. (5cm) piece of wire, and make a plain loop on one end. String a bicone, a rondelle, and a bicone on the

wire. Make a second loop in the same plane as the first **(photo c)**. Make a total of six bicone links.
[4] Open a jump ring (Basics), and slide three crystal teardrops onto it. Close the jump ring **(photo d)**. Make one more teardrop link.
[5] To make the focal dangle, cut 3 in. (7.6cm) of wire, and make half of a wrapped loop (Basics). Slide three teardrops into the loop **(photo e)**. Finish with two wraps **(photo f)**. Flatten the cut end with chainnose pliers. String a

c

d

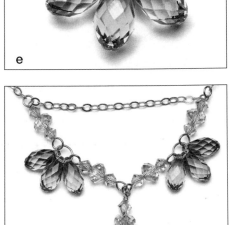

e

f

g

h

i

j

k

bicone, a rondelle, and a bicone on the long end. Make a wrapped loop above the bicone.

[6] Open one loop on two bicone links. Connect the bicone links to a teardrop link. Close the loops. Repeat to make a second set. Open the loop at one end of each set and connect them to the wrapped loop of the focal dangle made in step 5 **(photo g)**. Close the loops.

[7] Cut a 2-in. length of chain. Cut the remaining chain into two 9-in. (23cm) lengths. Open the loops at the ends of the unit made in step 6 and connect them with the 2-in. chain. Then attach a 9-in. chain to each loop **(photo h)**. Close the loops.

[8] Open both loops on a remaining bicone link. Attach one loop to the tenth chain link on one 9-in. chain, working from the connection made in step 7

(photo i). Skip ten chain links, and attach the other loop to the next link **(photo j)**. Close the loops. Repeat on the other end of the necklace.

[9] On the chains that parallel the bicone links, attach a short dangle to every other link **(photo k)**.

[10] On the 2-in. chain attached in step 7, attach the long dangle to the center link and connect a short dangle on each side. (Shorten the 2-in. chain if the dangles overlap the bicone links below it when you wear the necklace.)

[11] Open a jump ring, and attach the end chain link on one side of the necklace and a lobster claw clasp. Close the jump ring. Repeat on the other side of necklace, omitting the clasp.

MATERIALS

necklace 17 in. (43cm)
- crystals
  9 11 x 5.5mm teardrops
  8 6mm rondelles
  28 4mm bicones
- lobster claw clasp
- 15 in. (38cm) 22-gauge wire
- 20 in. (51cm) fine chain
- 13 1¼-in. (3.2cm) head pins, 22-gauge
- 4 6mm jump rings
- chainnose pliers
- roundnose pliers
- wire cutters

Lavender
lights

Bead artist Lea Zinke was first inspired to create these beads, her vision of hydrangeas in glass, by a trip to Cape Cod. They have now become her signature pieces.

by **Debbie Nishihara**

a

b

c

step*by*step

[1] Cut a 24-in. (61cm) piece of flexible beading wire (Basics, p. 8), and center the focal bead on it. String a 6º seed bead and a small daisy-shaped spacer on each side of the focal bead **(photo a)** to ensure that both sides of the necklace are balanced.
[2] String a pearl, a 10mm silver bead, and an 8mm citrine rondelle on one end.
[3] String a bead cap, an 18mm amethyst bead, and a bead cap **(photo b)**. String three pearls.
[4] String a star-shaped spacer, a 4mm bicone crystal, a 7mm citrine rondelle, a daisy spacer, a 10mm amethyst, a daisy spacer, a 7mm citrine rondelle, a bicone, and a star spacer. String three pearls.
[5] String a bead cap, a 15mm amethyst, a bead cap, and three pearls.
[6] Repeat step 4.
[7] Repeat steps 2–6 on the other side of the focal bead.
[8] String 12 pearls on each side. Adjust the length, if necessary, by adding or removing pearls.

[9] When the sides are uniform, string a daisy spacer, a 7mm amethyst, a star spacer, a 6º, a crimp bead, and a 6º on one end.
[10] String one half of a clasp and go back through the the beads strung in step 9. Pull the tail tight, and crimp the crimp bead (Basics and **photo c**).
[11] Repeat steps 9 and 10 on the other side. Trim the tails.

EDITOR'S NOTE:
This necklace uses several different sizes of faceted gemstones, but you may not be able to buy these beads individually in your area. Since strands can be expensive, try using the same size beads throughout or substituting gemstones with less expensive alternatives like simulated opals or faceted glass.

MATERIALS
necklace 21 in. (53cm)
• 38mm hydrangea or other focal bead (Lea Zinke, leazinke.com)
• 16-in. (41cm) strand 7mm faceted gold pearls
• faceted amethyst beads
  2 18mm
  2 15mm
  4 10mm
  2 7mm
• faceted citrine rondelles
  2 8mm
  8 7mm
• 8 4mm bicone crystals, lilac
• 6 size 6º seed beads, lavender
• 12 6mm daisy-shaped spacers
• 10 5mm star-shaped spacers
• toggle clasp
• 8 12mm bead caps
• 2 10mm silver beads
• 2 crimp beads
• flexible beading wire, size .019
• crimping pliers
• wire cutters

Falling star necklace

designed by **Sarah Ladiges**

Accentuate your neckline with this glittering choker. You can easily change the look of the necklace by adding different-sized dangles.

MATERIALS

necklace 16 in. (41cm)
- 15mm bead
- 4 11mm beads
- 6 5mm beads
- 4 6mm beads
- 68 4mm Czech fire-polished beads
- 34 3mm Czech fire-polished beads
- hook-and-eye clasp
- 15¼ in. (39cm) 22-gauge wire
- 6 1¼-in. (3.2cm) decorative head pins

- 16 in. (41cm) memory wire
- 30 in. (76cm) nylon beading thread or cord, size 0–1
- twisted wire beading needle
- G-S Hypo Cement
- chainnose pliers
- heavy-duty wire cutters (optional)
- roundnose pliers
- wire cutters

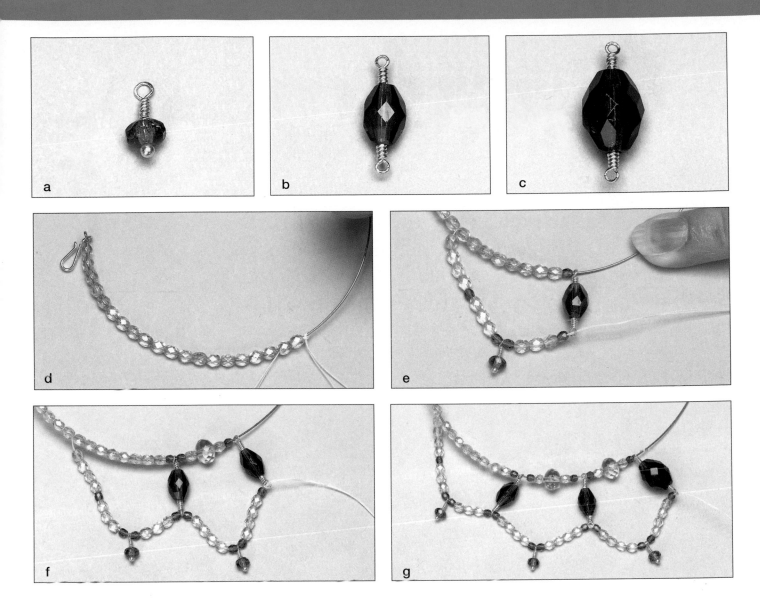

a

b

c

d

e

f

g

step*by*step

Components

[1] String a 5mm bead on a decorative head pin, and make a wrapped loop (Basics, p. 8) above the bead **(photo a)**. Make a total of six small dangles.

[2] Cut a 3-in. (7.6cm) piece of 22-gauge wire. Make a wrapped loop on one end. String an 11mm bead, and make a wrapped loop on the other side of the bead. Keep the loops in the same plane **(photo b)**. Repeat to make a total of four 11mm bead units.

[3] Cut a 3¼-in. (8.3cm) piece of 22-gauge wire, and make a wrapped loop on one end. String the 15mm accent bead, and make a wrapped loop on the other side of the bead **(photo c)**.

Necklace assembly

[1] Cut 16 in. (41cm) of memory wire (Basics) with heavy-duty wire cutters. Using roundnose pliers, roll the end of the memory wire to make a loop. Open the loop (Basics), attach half of a clasp, and close the loop. String 18 4mm beads on the wire.

[2] Cut 30 in. (76cm) of beading cord, and center it on a twisted wire beading needle. Pick up a 4mm bead, leaving a 1½-in. (3.8cm) tail of cord. String the bead on the wire.

[3] String a 4mm on the cord and on the wire. Make a half-hitch knot around the wire **(photo d and Basics)**. Repeat twice to add two more 4mms and knots.

[4] On the wire, string eight 4mms, a 3mm bead, and one loop of an 11mm bead unit. On the cord, string four 4mms, a 3mm, three 4mms, a 3mm, the loop of a wrapped dangle unit, a 3mm,

three 4mms, a 3mm, and the bottom loop of the 11mm bead unit **(photo e)**.

[5] On the wire, string a 3mm, a 4mm, a 6mm bead, a 4mm, a 3mm, and one loop of an 11mm bead unit. On the cord, string a 3mm, four or five 4mms (choose the amount that allows the best drape), a 3mm, a small dangle unit, a 3mm, four 4mms, a 3mm, and the bottom loop of the 11mm bead unit **(photo f)**.

[6] Repeat step 5, but add the 15mm bead unit instead of an 11mm bead unit **(photo g)**.

[7] String the second half of the necklace as a mirror image of the first half, securing the cord to the wire with several half-hitch knots. Seal the knots with G-S Hypo Cement, and trim the tails.

[8] Use roundnose pliers to roll the other end of the memory wire into a loop.

[9] Open the loop, attach the other half of the clasp, and close the loop.

Triple decker

Bead choice determines the flavor of this three-strand gemstone, pebble, and pearl necklace. Whichever beads you select, the key to unifying three dissimilar strands is to use one bead type in all of them.

designed by **Sibyl Rosen**

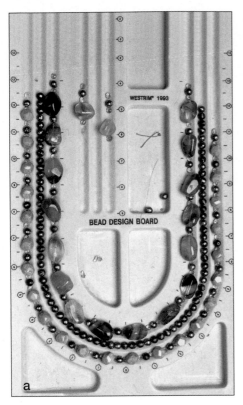

a

BEAD DESIGN BOARD

WESTRIM® 1993

b

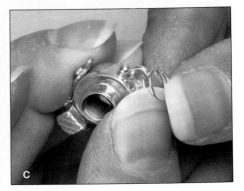

c

d

step*by*step

[1] Center 4 ft. (1.2m) of cord on a twisted wire beading needle. Tie the tails together with an overhand knot (Basics, p. 8), repeating in the same spot once or twice to make a bulky double or triple overhand knot.

[2] Glue the knot, trim the tails when dry, then string through a bead tip so the knot is inside it. Close the bead tip over the knot with chainnose pliers.

[3] Lay out the three strands on the design board, with the large pebble beads in the inner trough, the pearls in the center trough, and the gemstone or glass beads in the outer trough (photo a). Space out the pebbles with 6º seed beads, 3mm pearls, stone rondelles, or a combination of small beads (this strand is 19 in./48cm). The small bead strand is mostly pearls and uses the spacer beads from the pebble strand. Make it about ¾ in. (1.9cm) longer than the pebble strand. Space the medium-size gemstone beads in the outer trough with one or two of the spacers used in the pebble strand, and make this strand about 1½ in. (3.8cm) longer than the pebble strand.

[4] String the pebble strand on the prepared cord, then string a bead tip. Cut the cord at the fold, leaving the needle on one end, and string an 11º seed bead. Tie two surgeon's knots (Basics) around the seed bead (photo b). Glue the knot, trim the tails when dry, and close the bead tip.

[5] Repeat steps 1, 2, and 4 for the other two strands.

[6] Attach a split ring to each half of a clasp (photo c). Use roundnose pliers to roll the hooks of the bead tips around the split rings (photo d), attaching the ends of the three strands in the same order.

SUPPLY NOTE
Bead artist Judy Tamango created the porcelain "cave painting beads" in the tan and green necklace pictured to the left. Contact her via e-mail at coot17@comcast.net.

MATERIALS
necklace 21in. (53cm)
- 16-in. (41cm) strand large pebble beads
- 16-in. strand 6–10mm gemstone or glass beads
- 16-in. strand 5–6mm pearls or stone rondelles
- 16-in. strand 6–7mm pearls
- 150–200 size 6º seed beads or 3mm spacer beads
- 3–6 size 11º seed beads
- clasp
- 2 4–6mm split rings
- 6 bead tips
- 4 yd. (3.7m) nylon beading cord, size 2 or E
- twisted wire beading needles
- bead design board
- G-S Hypo Cement
- chainnose pliers
- roundnose pliers
- split-ring pliers (optional)

Shell lei

As you string this necklace, pay attention to each shell slice and how it fits against other shell slices and the jade. Try to arrange the shells so they fit nicely together, but make sure the jade can be seen between them.

by **Cheryl Phelan**

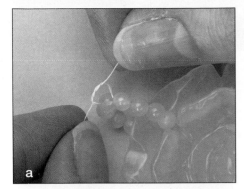

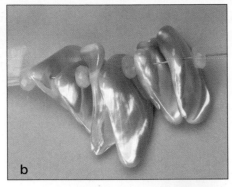

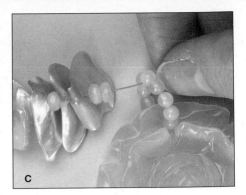

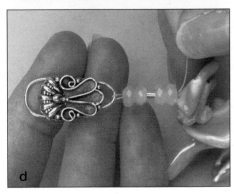

MATERIALS

necklace 17 in. (43cm)
- carved pendant, approx. 2 in. (5cm)
- 16-in. (41cm) strand mother-of-pearl shell slices
- 8–10 4mm round jade beads
- 42–48 3mm faceted jade rondelles
- clasp
- 2 crimp beads
- flexible beading wire, size .012–.014
- nylon beading thread, in a color to match 4mm round beads
- beading needles, #12
- G-S Hypo Cement
- crimping pliers
- clamp or tape
- wire cutters

step*by*step

[1] Attach a needle to 15 in. (38cm) of beading thread, and pick up four or five 4mm round jade beads, leaving a 5-in. (13cm) tail. Pass the needle through the hole on the carved pendant, and string four or five round beads. The number of beads in the loop will depend on how close to the necklace you'd like the pendant to hang. The loop for this necklace has nine beads.

[2] Tie the tail and the working thread together with a surgeon's knot (Basics, p. 8, and **photo a**) to form a loop. Retrace the thread path through the loop a few times. End both threads with half-hitch knots (Basics) between beads, and trim the excess thread. Dab the surgeon's knot with G-S Hypo Cement.

[3] Cut a 24-in. (61cm) piece of flexible beading wire (Basics) and string one jade rondelle and two shell slices. Continue stringing this pattern for the first half of the necklace (approx. 7 in./

18cm). Clamp or tape one end of the wire (**photo b**).

[4] String two jade rondelles on the beading wire and string the pendant loop over them (**photo c**). String the second half of the necklace to match the first.

[5] Test the necklace's fit. Allow an extra inch (2.5cm) for the four rondelles and crimp bead that you will add to each side, plus the length of the clasp. Remove the tape or clamp from the end, and add or remove beads from both ends as necessary.

[6] On one end, string two jade rondelles, a crimp bead, two jade rondelles and half of a clasp. Go back through the rondelles and the crimp (**photo d**). Crimp the crimp bead (Basics and **photo e**) and trim the excess wire. Repeat at the other end of the necklace.

Cool dip

Dip into your bead stash for crystals and seed beads in cool, refreshing colors. String them quickly and spend the rest of the day relaxing in your hammock.

designed by **Carol Pulk**

a

b

c

d

e

f

g

step*by*step

Necklace

[1] Determine the desired finished length of your necklace (this one is 17 in./43cm), and add 6 in. (15cm). Cut three pieces of flexible beading wire (Basics, p. 8) to that length.

[2] Center the following beads over all three wires: a 3mm crystal, an 11º seed bead, a 4mm crystal, an 11º, a 3mm, an 11º, a 4mm, an 11º, and a 3mm **(photo a)**.

[3] On one side of the necklace, string ten 11ºs, a 3mm, and ten 11ºs on each wire **(photo b)**.

[4] Over all three wires, string a bead cap, a 6mm bead, a flat spacer, a 10–12mm bead, a flat spacer, a 6mm bead, and a bead cap **(photo c)**.

[5] Separate the wires, and string 11ºs between a repeating pattern of a 3mm, an 11º, a 4mm, an 11º, and a 3mm. String about 5 in. (13cm) of beads, and adjust the placement of the crystal groups as you work so they are spaced randomly on the strands **(photo d)**.

[6] Repeat steps 3–5 on the other side of the necklace.

[7] Check the length, and adjust the number of beads on each strand as necessary. String a 4–6mm silver bead, a crimp bead, and one half of a clasp over all three wires on one end. Bring the wires back through the crimp and the silver bead **(photo e)**.

[8] Adjust the tension of the strands so the beads are snug, and crimp the crimp bead (Basics). Trim the excess wire.

[9] Repeat step 7 and 8 on the other end of the necklace.

Centerpiece

[1] String assorted glass beads, crystals, and silver beads on a head pin. Make a wrapped loop (Basics) above the beads.

[2] Make a total of five dangles, varying the bead combinations and length of each one. Before finishing the loops on three of the dangles, slide the end link of a ½–¾-in. (1.3–2cm) piece of chain into the loop **(photo f)**.

[3] Open the 6–8mm jump ring (Basics). Slide the dangles, chains, and charms onto it. Attach the jump ring to the center of the necklace **(photo g)** and close the jump ring.

MATERIALS

necklace 17 in. (43cm)
- 2 10–12mm glass beads
- 3–9 assorted glass beads and crystals for dangles
- 4 6mm glass beads
- 7–9 4–6mm silver beads
- 18–28 4mm bicone crystals
- 45–60 3mm bicone crystals
- 5g size 11º seed beads
- 4 5mm flat spacers
- 4 5mm bead caps
- silver charms
- toggle clasp
- 2 in. (5cm) chain
- 5 2-in. (5cm) head pins
- 6–8mm jump ring
- 2 crimp beads
- flexible beading wire, size .010
- chainnose pliers
- crimping pliers
- roundnose pliers
- wire cutters

Plaited pearls

Braided bead strands usually have a stiff look because braiding tightens the beads on the cords until they can no longer hang gracefully. The techniques described here solve that problem and result in a luscious necklace.

by **Alice Korach**

MATERIALS
necklace 18 in. (46cm)
- 2 6 x 9mm glass beads
- 2 16-in (41cm) strands 5mm pearls
- 2 16-in (41cm) strands 3 x 5mm stone beads
- size 11° seed beads
- 2 3mm silver beads
- toggle clasp
- 2 cones
- 6 in. (15cm) 20-gauge wire, half-hard or dead soft
- 6 yd. (5.4m) silk cord, size E
- 4 yd. (3.6m) nylon beading cord, size 1 or 2, or Fireline, 6 lb. test
- twisted wire beading needles
- G-S Hypo Cement
- awl (optional)
- chainnose pliers
- roundnose pliers
- tape
- wire cutters

EDITOR'S NOTE:
The trick to making a beautiful bead braid is to leave just the right amount of slack in the bead strands. You need enough slack to keep the beads from jamming together, but not so much that the beads separate on the strands, revealing unsightly cord.

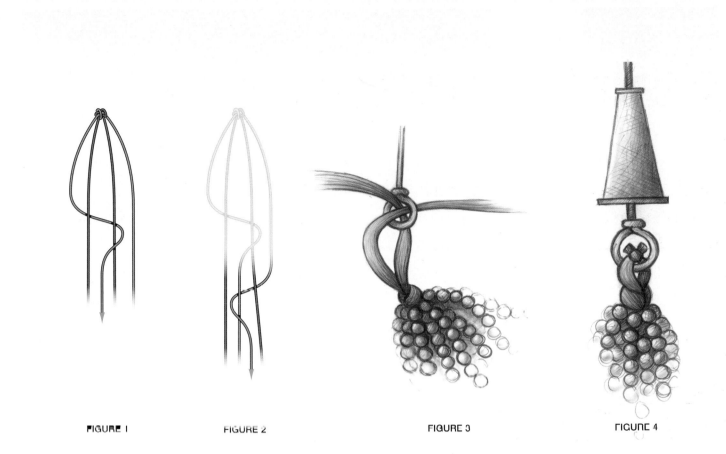

FIGURE 1   FIGURE 2   FIGURE 3   FIGURE 4

step*by*step

Preparing the strands

[1] Center a twisted wire beading needle on a 3-yd. (2.7m) length of silk cord. Tie an overhand knot (Basics, p. 8) about 4 in. (10cm) from the tails.
[2] String one strand of pearls on the cord. Slide the first pearl against the knot and make another overhand knot right against it. If necessary, slide an awl into the loop of the knot and use it to position the knot against the pearl. When the knot is tight against the pearl, let it slip off the tip of the awl. Continue in this manner until you have knotted between each pearl and after the last one.
[3] Repeat steps 1 and 2 with the other strand of pearls.
[4] Cut a 2-yd. (1.8m) piece of beading cord or Fireline, and prepare it as in step 1.
[5] Alternately string an 11º seed bead and a 3 x 5mm stone bead until you have strung a complete strand of stone beads. End with an 11º. Tie an over-hand knot about ¼ in. (6mm) past the last bead.
[6] Repeat with the other strand of stone beads.

Making the braid

[1] String one set of tails from all four strands through a 6 x 9mm glass beads, and tape them together or tie a loose overhand knot.
[2] Position the strands so the pearls are on the outside and the stones are in the center, and work a four-strand braid: Cross the far left strand behind the next two strands. Come out between the two right-hand strands, and cross back over the second strand from the right. It is now the inside-left strand **(figure 1)**.

Cross the far right strand behind the next two strands on the left. Come out between the two left-hand strands, and cross back over the second strand from the left. It is now the inside-right strand **(figure 2)**.

Alternate these two motions for the length of the strands.
[3] When you've braided to the other end, pass all the thread tails through the other glass bead.

Finishing

[1] Cut a 3-in. piece of wire, and make a wrapped loop (Basics) on one end.
[2] Making sure all the strands are pulled up against the 6 x 9mm bead, pass half of the tails through the wrapped loop from front to back and the other half through from back to front **(figure 3)**. Tie two surgeon's knots (Basics), trim the tails, and dot with G-S Hypo Cement. Repeat on the other end.
[3] Pull the wire into a cone **(figure 4)**, string a 3mm silver bead on the wire, and make the first half of a wrapped loop. Attach the loop of one half of a clasp, and complete the wraps.
[4] Repeat steps 1–3, using the other half of the clasp, to finish the other side of the necklace.

Tiered drops

Simple
wraps
secure
dangling
pearls and
crystals in a
project inspired
by a necklace
worn by actress
Cate Blanchett
in the historical
drama *Elizabeth*.

designed by **Annie Corkill**

a

b

c

d

e

f

g

step*by*step

Dangles

[1] On a head pin, string a pearl and a 4mm bicone crystal. Make a wrapped loop (Basics, p. 8, and **photo a**). Repeat to make a total of 17 small dangles, and set them aside.

[2] String two pearls on a head pin or a decorative head pin and make a wrapped loop (**photo b**). Repeat to make a total of 16 pearl components.

[3] String a 6mm bicone crystal and a 4mm bicone crystal on a head pin. Make the first half of a wrapped loop, slide a pearl component into the loop (**photo c**), and finish the wraps. Repeat to make a total of eight compound bicone dangles.

[4] Repeat step 3. Use a 6mm round crystal instead of a 6mm bicone (**photo d**). Make a total of eight compound round dangles.

Necklace base

[1] Make a wrapped loop at one end of 2 ft. (61cm) of 24-gauge wire.

[2] String a pearl, the loop of one small dangle, and a pearl (**photo e**).

[3] String a compound round dangle by wrapping the wire between the two pearls (**photo f**).

[4] Repeat step 2.

[5] Repeat step 3 using a compound bicone dangle (**photo g**).

h

i

[6] Repeat steps 2–5 seven times.

[7] String a pearl, the loop of one small dangle, and a pearl.

[8] Make a wrapped loop on the end of the wire.

Adjustable chain ends

[1] Open a jump ring (Basics), and attach it to a wrapped loop at one end of the wire and 1 in. (2.5cm) of chain (**photo h**). Close the jump ring.

[2] Open a jump ring, and attach a lobster claw clasp to the other end of the chain. Close the jump ring.

[3] Repeat step 1 at the other end of the necklace using 3 in. (7.6cm) of chain.

[4] String a pearl and a 4mm bicone on a head pin, and make a wrapped loop. Repeat to make a second dangle.

[5] Use a jump ring to attach the two dangles to the chain (**photo i**).

MATERIALS

choker 12½–15 in. (32–38cm)

- 85 6mm round pearls
- Swarovski crystals
  35 4mm bicones
  8 6mm bicones
  8 6mm rounds
- lobster claw clasp
- 2 ft. (61cm) 24-gauge wire
- 4 in. (10cm) chain with 4mm links
- 51 2-in. (5cm) head pins, or 35 2-in. (5cm) head pins and **16** decorative head pins
- 4 4mm jump rings
- chainnose pliers
- roundnose pliers
- wire cutters

Sparkling sunflowers

Use petal-shaped cubic zirconias and glittering crystals to weave a cheerful, flower-shaped pendant.

designed by **May Brisebois**

MATERIALS

choker 15 in. (38cm)
- 8mm round crystal, smoky topaz
- 8 7 x 10mm petal (saddle-shaped) cubic zirconia beads, color B (Beadiful, beadifulgifts.com)
- 8 5mm bicone crystals, color A
- 4mm bicone crystals
  8 color A
  18 color B
- 4g size 11º seed beads
- 1mm crimp bead
- bail with loop
- cup-style bead tip
- monofilament 10 lb. test; or flexible beading wire, .012
- memory wire, necklace diameter
- chainnose pliers
- heavy-duty wire cutters (for memory wire)
- roundnose pliers
- wire cutters (for flexible beading wire)

stepbystep

Pendant

The flatter side of the petal-shaped cubic zirconia beads will be referred to as the front of the bead, while the other side will be the back.

[1] Center eight 11º seed beads on 1 yd. (.9m) of monofilament or beading wire. Using one end, go through the first bead, and pull tight to form a ring (photo a).
[2] With the left end of the wire, pick up a 4mm color A bicone crystal, a petal-shaped cubic zirconia bead (CZ) (sewing front to back), a 5mm bicone crystal, a CZ (sewing back to front), and an A. With the same end and working clockwise around the ring of 11ºs, go through the next 11º (photo b and figure 1, a–b).

With the other end, go through the last two beads picked up in the opposite direction (photo c and figure 1, c–d). Pull tight.

[3] Continuing with the end exiting the CZ, pick up a 5mm, a CZ (sewing back to front), and an A. Go through the next 11º in the ring (figure 2, a–b). With the other end, go through the last two beads picked up in the opposite direction (c–d). Pull tight.
[4] Repeat step 3, working around the ring, until you've added eight CZs.
[5] To join the first and last petals, use the end exiting the eighth CZ to pick up a 5mm (figure 3, a–b). With the end exiting the 11º, go through the first two beads picked up in step 2 (figure 3, c–d), and cross through the 5mm just added (photo d and figure 3, d–e).
[6] With each end, continue through the next four 5mms, crossing through the opposite 5mm (photo e). Pull tight to form the flower's base.
[7] With both ends together, pick up an 8mm round crystal. Cross the ends through the 5mm opposite where the ends are exiting. Continue with each wire end through the 5mms, and exit

a

b

c

d

e

f

g

FIGURE 1

FIGURE 2

FIGURE 3

FIGURE 4

between two crystals on the other side (figure 4, a–b and c–d).

[8] Over both ends, pick up two 11⁰s, a bead tip, and a crimp bead (**photo f**). Pull tight, and using chainnose pliers, flatten the crimp bead. Trim the ends. Using roundnose pliers, close the bead tip.

[9] Attach the loop of the bead tip to the loop of a bail. Using roundnose pliers, close the loop, securing it to the bail (**photo g**).

Choker

[1] Cut 16 in. (41cm) of memory wire (Basics, p. 8) using heavy-duty wire cutters. Center the bail of the pendant, and pick up ten 11⁰s on each end.

[2] On each end, pick up a 4mm color B bicone crystal, five 11⁰s, a B, five 11⁰s, a B, and 20 11⁰s. Repeat twice. Check the fit and add or remove beads as necessary.

[3] On each end, use roundnose pliers to form a small loop close to the beads. Trim any excess memory wire.

Some assembly required

Make an easy and playful necklace that looks more complex than it really is. Best of all, you can make it with almost any small beads you have on hand.

designed by **Wendy Witchner**

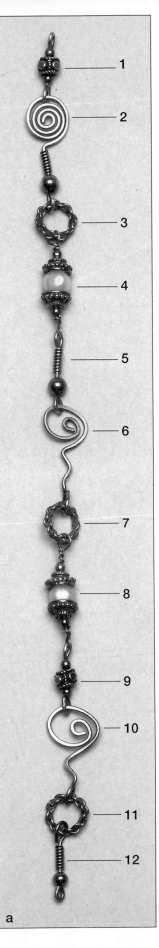

a

b

step*by*step

Components

[1] Cut one 1-in. (2.5cm), four 2¼-in. (5.7cm), and two 3-in. (7.6cm) pieces of 20-gauge wire. Use the 1-in. (2.5cm) piece to make a hook following the template in **figure 1**.

[2] Shape the 2¼-in. pieces following the template in **figure 2**, turning a small loop perpendicular to the coil at the straight end of each one.

[3] Shape the 3-in. pieces following the template in **figure 3** but leaving the straight end unfinished. String a coil or tube-shaped bead and a 3mm bead on the straight end of each piece. Trim the excess wire to ⅜ in. (1cm) above the end bead and turn a plain loop (photo a – component 2) perpendicular to the coil.

[4] Hammer both sides of the shaped sections of all these pieces to harden them.

[5] Cut eight 1-in. pieces of 22-gauge wire. Turn a plain loop (Basics, p. 8) on one end of each. String a 3mm bead and a wire coil or tube-shaped bead on four of them. Finish with another plain loop (photo a – components 5 and 12).

[6] On the end of the remaining wires cut in step 2, string a 2mm bead, a spacer, and another 2mm bead. Trim the excess wire to ⅜ in., and finish with another plain loop (photo a – 1 and 9).

[7] Cut five 2-in. (5cm) pieces of 22-gauge wire. Make the first half of a wrapped loop on one end of four of these wires (Basics). String each one with a 2mm, a bead cap (narrow end first), an 8mm pearl, bead cap (wide end first), and 2mm. Make the first half of a wrapped loop close to the end bead (photo a – 4 and 8).

[8] With the remaining wire cut in step 7, make the pendant. Strike one end with your hammer to form a small paddle that will keep a 2mm from falling off. Trim the paddle with wire cutters, if desired, to refine its shape, and file it until the edges are smooth.

String a 2mm, a 10mm pearl, a bead cap, and a 2mm. Trim the excess wire to ⅜ in. (1cm) above the end bead, and make a loop (photo b).

Necklace assembly

[1] Lay out the components for each side of the necklace as shown in **photo a** or in the sequence you desire. Place jump rings between several of the components (photo a – 3, 7, and 11).

[2] Cut two ½-in. (1.3cm) pieces of chain. Open the loop on the pendant (Basics) and attach it to an end link on each piece of chain. Close the loops.

[3] Attach the first necklace component (photo a – 1) to one chain attached to the pendant. Continue adding components to each side of the necklace until you've attached all the components and jump rings. Finish the wrapped loops of the components made in step 7 after attaching them. Vary the sequence as you like, but keep the components in the same order on each side of the necklace.

[4] Cut the remaining chain in half. Attach one piece of chain to the end component on each side. Attach a clasp hook to the end link of one chain segment. If desired, add a split ring to the end link on the other chain segment.

MATERIALS

necklace 18 in. (46cm)
- 10mm freshwater pearl
- 4 8mm freshwater pearls
- 4 4mm silver beads
- 7 3mm round beads
- 18 2mm round beads
- 6 ³⁄₁₆-in. (5mm) wire coils or tube-shaped beads
- 9 bead caps to fit pearls
- 20 in. (51cm) 20-gauge wire, dead soft
- 20 in. (51cm) 22-gauge wire, dead soft
- 7 in. (18cm) chain
- 10 8mm decorative or twisted wire soldered jump rings
- 6mm split ring (optional)
- anvil
- chainnose pliers
- hammer
- metal file
- roundnose pliers
- wire cutters

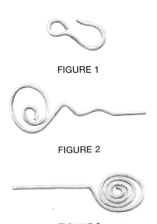

FIGURE 1

FIGURE 2

FIGURE 3

Multistrand elegance

This elegant multistrand necklace can be as expensive or inexpensive as you like — you control the cost through your selection of beads. This version pairs Czech glass beads with Czech fire-polished beads so it's easy on the wallet and the eye.

designed by **Terri Torbeck**

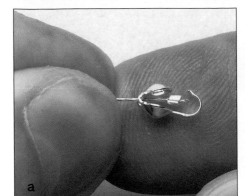

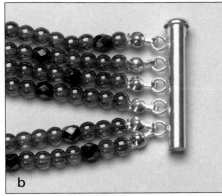

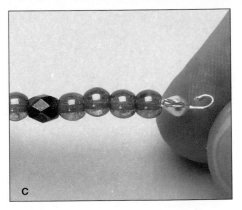

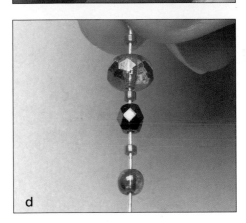

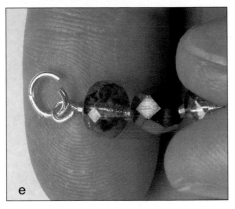

step*by*step

Strands

[1] Cut five 16-in. (41cm) pieces of flexible beading wire (Basics, p. 8) and one 19-in. (48cm) piece.

[2] With crimping pliers, crimp a crimp bead (Basics) near the end of one wire, and string it through a bead tip (photo a). Trim the excess wire, and use chainnose pliers to close the bead tip around the crimp bead.

[3] String a mixture of 4mm fire-polished beads and 4mm round glass beads, randomly spacing fire-polished beads every three to seven glass beads (photo b). Stop 1½ in. (3.8cm) from the other end of the strand. Snug up the beads. Clamp or tape the wire ends.

[4] Repeat steps 2 and 3 to make a total of six strands. As you're stringing, check the position of the fire-polished beads in the strands in relation to each other. If they line up vertically, respace them.

[5] Pass the bead tip hook on one short strand through the top loop on one half of a clasp. Roll the hook closed with round-nose pliers. Repeat with the remaining short strands, attaching one per loop.

[6] Remove the clamp or tape from one end of the longest strand, and attach it to the bottom loop of the clasp. With a five-loop clasp, this strand shares a loop with a short strand.

[7] Remove the clamp or tape from the other end of the strands. Snug the beads and make sure the short strands are all exactly the same length.

[8] Slide on a bead tip so the hook faces away from the beads. String a crimp bead, snug it inside the bead tip, and crimp it with chainnose pliers. Trim the excess wire and close the bead tip (photo c). Repeat with the remaining strands.

Beaded dangle

[1] String a 4mm bead, an 11º cylinder bead, a 5mm fire-polished bead, an 11º, a rondelle, an 11º, a 5mm crystal, an 11º, a rondelle, and an 11º (photo d) on a head pin. Make a plain loop above the beads (Basics).

[2] Open the jump ring (Basics), and attach it to the loop on the dangle (photo e). Close the loop. Slide the jump ring onto the longest strand (photo f).

Finishing

Attach the strands to the other half of the clasp as in steps 5 and 6 of "Strands."

MATERIALS

necklace 15 in. (38cm) (the bottom strand is 3 in./7.6cm longer)
• 2 4 x 6mm faceted glass rondelles
• 5mm Czech fire-polished bead
• 5 16-in. (41cm) strands 4mm round Czech glass beads
• 2 8-in. (20cm) strands 4mm Czech fire-polished beads
• 5 size 11º cylinder beads
• slide clasp, 5 or 6 loops
• 2 in. (5cm) head pin
• 6mm jump ring
• 12 crimp beads
• 12 bead tips
• flexible beading wire, size .012–.014
• chainnose pliers
• clamps or tape
• crimping pliers
• roundnose pliers

Pearls and gems

Play off color and shape with luscious stick pearls and stone slices.

designed by **Kelly Charveaux**

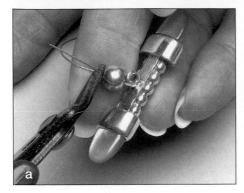

a

b

c

step*by*step

[1] Cut a 40-in. (1m) length of flexible beading wire (Basics, p. 8). String a crimp bead and the loop of one half of a clasp, and take the tail back through the crimp bead. Flatten the crimp with chainnose pliers (Basics). Slide a large-hole silver bead over both wires and the crimp, and trim the tail at the bottom of the large-hole bead **(photo a)**.

[2] String about 32 in. (81cm) of beads in an alternating pattern, not going more than seven beads before repeating the first bead. It's fine to have two stone slices or pearls separated by a silver spacer bead. Just don't repeat any given pattern too often.

[3] It's a little tricky to crimp tightly enough and still conceal the crimp. For best results, string the second large hole bead, then a crimp bead, and the other half of the clasp, and go back through the crimp and the large-hole bead. Tighten all the beads on the strand and the loop through the clasp, leaving just enough slack to push the crimp part of the way above the large-hole bead **(photo b)**. You may have to use an awl. Flatten the crimp with chainnose pliers — the tip of the pliers should be inside the large-hole bead **(photo c)** — and cut off the excess wire flush with the bottom of the large-hole bead.

[4] Finally, redistribute the small amount of slack back into the necklace so the large-hole bead covers the crimp.

MATERIALS
necklace 34 in. (86cm)
- 16-in. (41cm) strand 22–40mm stick pearls
- 16-in. (41cm) strand 22–40mm tumbled stone slices
- 16-in. (41cm) strand 5–8mm pearls, round or coin shaped, in one or more colors
- 50–75 3 x 5mm–5 x 8mm tooled Thai silver beads
- 2 4mm large-hole beads
- toggle clasp
- 2 crimp beads
- flexible beading wire, .014–.015
- awl (optional)
- chainnose pliers
- wire cutters

SUPPLY NOTES:
- Irregular pearls offer a variety of shapes and hues and a natural look, but they don't come cheap. Stringing them with tumbled stones will make a 16-in. (41cm) strand go further and set them off to best advantage.
- Center-drilled stick pearls can be found at pearlbeadsale.com.

Modern clusters

Wrap crystals, pearls, glass, and gemstones through geometric links for a necklace with casual elegance.

designed by **Irina Miech**

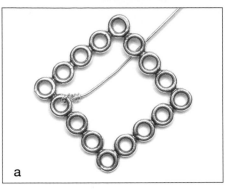

a

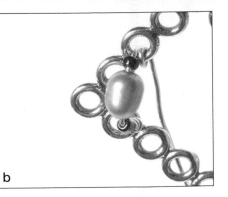

b

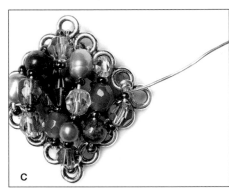

c

d

MATERIALS

necklace 18 in. (46cm)

- 40–50 3–8mm crystals, pearls, or other accent beads
- 3g 13° Charlotte seed beads
- 18 x 18mm geometric cluster link
- lobster claw or hook clasp with soldered jump ring or extender chain
- 10 in. (25cm) 24-gauge wire, dead soft
- 1–2 1-in. (2.5cm) head pins
- 4 crimp beads
- flexible beading wire, .015
- chainnose pliers
- crimping pliers
- roundnose pliers
- wire cutters

EDITOR'S NOTE:

As you weave the wire through the link, work slowly to avoid kinks. Carefully position each wrap before pulling the wire tight around the loops.

step*by*step

Pendant

[1] Cut a 10-in. (25cm) piece of 24-gauge wire, and make the first half of a wrapped loop (Basics, p. 8) at one end. Attach the wrapped loop to the inner edge of a loop next to a corner loop on the link, and complete the wraps **(photo a)**.

[2] Pick up a 13° Charlotte, an accent bead, and a Charlotte, and pass the wire through the second loop on the other side of the corner loop. Go through the loop a second time to make a wrap **(photo b)**.

[3] Flip the link over, and pick up an alternating pattern of Charlottes and accent beads to reach the next loop on the side you started on. Go through the loop twice to make a wrap.

[4] Repeat step 3 until you reach the loop next to the corner loop opposite where you started. Pass the wire through the loop, and make two wraps around the wire, as in a wrapped loop **(photo c)**.

[5] On a head pin, string an accent bead, a Charlotte, an accent bead, a Charlotte, and an accent bead, and make the first half of a wrapped loop. Determine the bottom loop for your pendant, attach the dangle to this loop, and complete the wraps **(photo d)**. Trim the excess wire.

Necklace

[1] Determine where on your pendant you will attach the two beaded strands.

[2] Cut 12 in. (30cm) of beading wire (Basics), and string a crimp bead and one of the loops of the pendant. Go back through the crimp bead, and crimp it (Basics and **photo e**).

[3] String 2–2½ in. (5–6.4cm) of accent beads separated by groups of Charlottes, then string 5½ in. (14cm) of Charlottes.

[4] String a crimp bead and half of a clasp, and go back through the crimp bead.

[5] Repeat steps 2–3 on the other side of the pendant. Repeat step 4, substituting a jump ring or extender chain for the clasp. Check the fit, add or remove beads from each end if necessary, crimp the crimp beads, and trim.

[6] To add an optional dangle to the extender chain, string an accent bead on a head pin, and make the first half of a wrapped loop. Attach the loop to the last link of the extender chain, complete the wraps, and trim (**photo f**).

DESIGNER'S TIP:
Geometric links are available in different shapes and sizes, so have fun playing with the options!

Better in blue

When working with a large single-color focal piece, such as this dramatic dichroic pendant, it can be hard to match the color with one strand of complementary beads. By using five strands of seed beads dressed up with a few crystals, simulated opals, and silver, you can pick up several of the shades in the pendant, creating a necklace that won't overpower it.

by **Debbie Nishihara**

MATERIALS

necklace 19½ in. (49.5cm)

- blue focal piece or pendant with bail
- 16-in. (41cm) strand 6mm synthetic opals
- 16-in. strand 5mm royal blue faceted cat's eye beads
- crystals, sapphire
  - 2 5mm bicones
  - 24 4mm bicones
- seed beads
  - hank size 11º, royal blue
  - hank size 12º 3-cut, purple/blue
  - 50 size 8º silver-lined white
- 10 10mm sterling silver saucer beads
- 52 4mm daisy-shaped silver spacers
- 132 3mm daisy-shaped silver spacers
- toggle clasp
- 2 silver cones
- 6 in. (15cm) 22-gauge wire
- 4–6 silver crimp beads
- flexible beading wire, size .014
- chainnose pliers
- roundnose pliers
- clamps or tape
- wire cutters

a

b

step*by*step

Setting up

[1] Cut two 3-in. (7.6cm) pieces of 22-gauge wire. (Your wires should be 2 in./5cm longer than your cones to leave room for wrapped loops.)

[2] Make a wrapped loop at one end of each wire (Basics, p. 8).

[3] This necklace is 19 in. (48cm) long without the clasp. Cut five 22-in. (56cm) pieces of flexible beading wire (Basics). If you find it's easier to pull the wires through the crimps when you've got lots left over, allow for those extra inches now.

Stringing patterns

[1] On all five wires center a 5mm bicone crystal, a 4mm spacer, an opal, a saucer bead, an opal, the pendant, an opal, a saucer bead, an opal, a 4mm spacer, and a 5mm crystal (photo a).

[2] Choose a strand on one side of the pendant, and string ten 11º seed beads, and then the following pattern: 3mm spacer, 8º seed bead, 3mm spacer, ten 11ºs, 4mm spacer, cat's eye, silver

EDITOR'S NOTE:

When stringing into cones, adjust your bead counts so you don't waste spacers or expensive beads by hiding them.

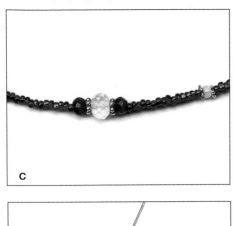

c

d

e

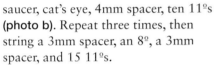

f

g

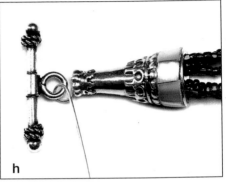

h

saucer, cat's eye, 4mm spacer, ten 11ºs (photo b). Repeat three times, then string a 3mm spacer, an 8º, a 3mm spacer, and 15 11ºs.

[3] Choose a new strand, and string the following pattern: 15 11ºs, cat's eye, 4mm spacer, opal, 4mm spacer, cat's eye, 15 11ºs, 3mm spacer, 8º, 3mm spacer (photo c). Repeat three times, then string five 11ºs.

[4] Repeat step 3 with another strand.

[5] Choose a fourth strand, and string the following pattern: three 3-cut seed beads, 3mm spacer, 4mm bicone crystal, 3mm spacer, 15 3-cuts. Then string the following pattern: 3mm spacer, 8º, 3mm spacer, 15 3-cuts, 3mm spacer, 4mm crystal, 3mm spacer, 15 3-cuts (photo d). Repeat twice, then string a 3mm spacer, an 8º, a 3mm spacer, and 25 3-cuts.

[6] Repeat step 5 with the remaining strand. Clamp or tape the wires' ends.

[7] Repeat steps 2–6 to string the other side of the necklace as a mirror image of the first.

Finishing

[1] Check the fit, and add or remove beads as necessary so both sides are even. By adjusting the bead counts at the ends, you can stagger the placement of the opals and other elements exiting the cone (photo e).

[2] Gather the ends from one side of the necklace, and remove the clamps or tape. String at least two strands through a crimp bead, the wrapped loop created in step 2 of "Setting up," and back through the crimp bead. You may string all five strands through one crimp bead (photo f), but multiple crimp beads may be preferable and won't be visible inside the cones. Because the strands tend to slip here, you may want to hold the necklace up and pull each wire through individually with a pair of pliers before crimping. Pull the strands tight, crimp the crimp bead(s), and trim the tails.

[3] Repeat step 2 with the other side of the necklace.

[4] Slide a cone over the wire, and pull the strands all the way in (photo g).

[5] Make the first half of a wrapped loop, and attach one half of a clasp (photo h). Finish the loop, and trim the end of the wire.

[6] Repeat steps 4 and 5 on the other end of the necklace, using the other half of the clasp.

EDITOR'S NOTE:
Finished jewelry should end with a bang. The person who wears your work will appreciate you going that extra step to finish your pieces with unique and beautiful findings.

Crystal drop necklace

Crystal drops and seed beads
turn this simple pattern into a
versatile necklace that will work
for dinner and a movie or an
elegant formal affair.

designed by **Erika Frost**

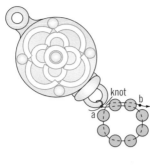

FIGURE 1

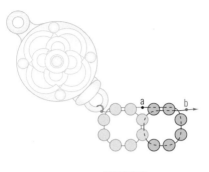

FIGURE 2

MATERIALS

necklace 16 in. (41cm)
- 15 5 x 11mm crystal or Czech glass drops
- 3g size 11º seed beads
- box clasp
- beading thread or Fireline 6 lb. test
- beading needles, #12
- G-S Hypo Cement

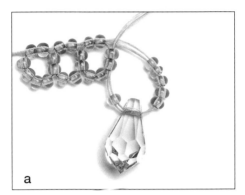

a

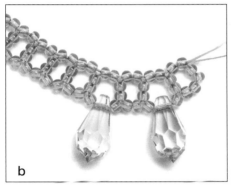

b

EDITOR'S NOTE

Your choice of colors in this versatile necklace will help determine whether it's best with casual or formal wear. Try making a version in bright colors to add a little sparkle to jeans; try white or clear crystals (above) to pair with a more elegant dress.

step*by*step

[1] Thread a needle with a comfortable length of beading thread or Fireline. Sew through the loop on one half of a clasp, and tie several square knots (Basics, p. 8), leaving an 8-in. (20cm) tail. Dot the knots with G-S Hypo Cement, and let the glue dry.

[2] Pick up eight 11º seed beads, and sew through the first two 11ºs again to form a ring (figure 1, a–b).

[3] Pick up six 11ºs. Sew through two 11ºs on the ring and the first two new beads (figure 2, a–b).

[4] Repeat step 3 for 5 in. (13cm) for a 16-in. (41cm) necklace, 6 in. (15cm) for an 18-in. (46cm) necklace, and 7 in. (18cm) for a 20-in. (51cm) necklace. Each ring will have two 11ºs on each side.

[5] To add the crystal drops, string five 11ºs, a drop, and an 11º.

[6] Sew through two 11ºs on the previous ring (photo a) and the first two 11ºs of the new ring, as before. Instead of having two 11ºs on the bottom edge of the ring, there will be an 11º, a drop, and an 11º.

[7] Alternate plain and drop rings (photo b). String a total of 15 rings with drops.

[8] Stitch the remainder of the necklace without drops, making the second side the same length as the first section.

[9] When you reach the end, tie the thread to the other half of the clasp as in step 1, but do not cut the thread. Sew back through the first ring, and secure the thread using a half-hitch knot (Basics). Repeat with one or two more half-hitch knots. Sew through a few beads, and trim the thread.

[10] Secure the tail on the other half of the clasp as in step 9. Glue the knots.

Midnight lariat

This lariat is noticeably different than most: it's short, measuring a mere 23 in. (58cm) from end to end, and keeps its appeal close to the neckline. If you feel overwhelmed wearing yards of beads, try this classy, compact version.

by **Mindy Brooks**

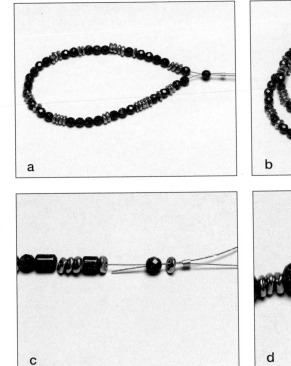

a

b

c

d

SUPPLY NOTE:
The sparkling midnight-blue beads that give this lariat its distinctive luster are called blue goldstones. They're actually glass, not stone, and the flecks that appear to be gold are copper crystals. The beads are imported from Italy. You can find them both plain and faceted and in different shapes and sizes.

MATERIALS
necklace 23 in. (58cm)
• 15–20mm focal bead
• 5 16-in. (40cm) strands 4mm blue goldstones
• 3 16-in. strands brass spacer beads
• 8 2mm beads or 11º seed beads, blue or gold
• 18 crimp beads
• 4 yd. (3.7m) flexible beading wire, .013–.014
• chainnose or crimping pliers
• clamps or tape

step*by*step

[1] Cut two 52-in. (1.25m) lengths of flexible beading wire (Basics, p. 8). Center 7 in. (18cm) of 4mm blue goldstone and 3mm brass spacer beads on each wire in whatever pattern you choose. Bend one strand in half, and, over both wire ends, string a 4mm and a crimp bead **(photo a)**. Repeat with the other strand. Crimp the crimp beads (Basics). Stagger them slightly, if necessary, so they'll fit inside the focal bead.
[2] String the focal bead over all four wire ends **(photo b)**.
[3] String a random pattern of beads on each wire end, stopping about 7 in. from the end. Secure the beads temporarily with clamps or tape.
[4] To create the eight-strand fringe, add a short piece of wire to the end of each beaded strand as follows: Cut four 7-in. pieces of beading wire. Lay one short piece next to the exposed wire at the end of a strand, aligning the bottoms. Remove the clamp or tape from the beaded strand, and string both wires with several beads and a crimp **(photo c)**. Slide the beads into place and crimp the

crimp. Repeat with the rest of the wire ends, varying the crimp placement on each strand.
[5] String approximately 4 in. (10cm) of beads on each of the eight fringe strands, adding a crimp among the last few beads. String a 2mm or 11º seed bead on the end of each strand. Skip the end bead, and string the wire back through a few beads, exiting one bead past the crimp **(photo d)**. Tighten the wire, but allow enough ease so the fringe hangs gracefully. Crimp the crimp, and trim the wire. Repeat with the remaining strands.

Focal bead fun

Set off a large focal bead with a spray of accent beads in a multistrand necklace. Natural cord lends a casual elegance to the classic look of pearls, or, if you prefer, a large art-glass bead nestles harmoniously within colored strands.

designed by **Ludmila Raitzin**

a

b

c

d

e

step*by*step

[1] Cut 60 23-in. (58cm) and two 46-in. (1.2m) pieces of hemp cord. Fold the long strands in half, and lay them out, loops opposite each other **(photo a)**. Lay the rest of the strands on top of the folded strands. Gather the strands on one end, including the folded loop, and align the ends. Secure the strands with a rubber band ¾ in. (1.9cm) from the end **(photo b)**.

[2] Cut a 6-in. (15cm) piece of wire. Make the first half of a wrapped loop (Basics, p. 8) on one end. Slide the cord loop into the wire loop, and finish the wraps **(photo c)**.

[3] Tie an 18-in. (46cm) piece of thread around the gathered strands ⅛ in. (3mm) from the end. Wrap the thread around the end several times to secure the strands. Secure the thread with a square knot (Basics), thread a needle on each tail, and sew into the wraps. Trim the tails.

[4] Dot the cord ends with glue **(photo d)**, and allow them to dry. Remove the rubber band.

[5] Above the wrapped loop, string an end cap or cone and an accent bead. Make the first half of a wrapped loop, attach a lobster claw clasp, and finish the wraps **(photo e)**.

MATERIALS

necklace 17 in. (43cm)
- 22mm focal bead
- 124 5–6mm pearls with large holes, or crystals
- 2 4mm accent beads
- lobster claw clasp
- 2 15mm cones or end caps
- 12 in. (30cm) 20–22-gauge wire, half-hard
- 2 in. (5cm) chain with links large enough to accommodate clasp
- nylon beading thread
- 41 yd. (37m) 20 lb. hemp cord
- beading needles, #12
- cyanoacrylate glue
- rubber bands
- scissors
- bead reamer (optional)
- chainnose pliers
- roundnose pliers
- wire cutters

f

g

h

i

[6] Separate 1⁄ strands of cord, including the loop of the unfinished end, and make an overhand knot (Basics) 4 in. (10cm) from the cone **(photo f)**. String a focal bead on one of the strands (or on more strands if the bead's hole allows it), and slide it up to the knot **(photo g)**.

[7] Make an overhand knot with all the strands so the focal bead is snug between the two knots **(photo h)**.

[8] Dot the end of each strand with glue, allow them to dry, and trim each one diagonally. String two 6mm pearls or crystals on each strand **(photo i)**. If the holes of the pearls are too small, use a bead reamer to enlarge them.

[9] Gather all the ends, and secure them with a rubber band. Align each strand with the cord loop, trimming each strand to remove the glued end. Repeat steps 2–5 to complete the necklace, using chain instead of the clasp in step 5.

SUPPLY NOTE:
As an alternative to these designs, try colored cord embellished with glass and crystal beads that add sparkle to each strand. You could also use leather, silk, or cotton cord and wood, bone, or other natural beads to complement the design.

EDITOR'S NOTE:
Cord sometimes comes wrapped around cards and can be kinky when unwrapped. To take out the kinks, cut the strands to length, run them under warm water, and lay them out flat until they dry.

Pearl garden

Create a stunning pearl
necklace from a collection
of sparkling components.
The luminescence of these
pale, rose-colored stick pearls is
reflected by faceted crystals and
fire-polished beads.

designed by **Christine Strube**

MATERIALS

necklace 18 in. (46cm)

- 16-in. (41cm) strand of pearls
  stick pearls, pink
  10mm coin pearls, white
  8mm oval pearls, silver
  4mm round pearls, mauve
- 13 8mm round cloisonné beads, color
  to match pearls
- fire-polished beads
  9 8mm faceted round, rose
  4 6mm faceted round, rose
  2 4mm faceted round, pink
- crystals
  21 4mm bicones, lt. Colorado topaz AB
- 42 5mm daisy-shaped spacers
- 10 2mm round silver beads
- 22.5mm lobster claw clasp
- 2 in. (5cm) large-link cable chain
- 65 3 in. (7.6cm) head pins
- 2 crimp beads
- flexible beading wire, .012–.014
- chainnose pliers
- crimping pliers
- file (optional)
- wire cutters

step*by*step

Dangles

[1] Stack a 5mm spacer, a 6mm faceted rondelle, a spacer, and a 4mm bicone on a head pin (**photo a**). Make 15.
[2] Stack a 4mm pearl and a rondelle on a head pin (**photo b**). Make 14.
[3] Stack a 2mm silver bead, a spacer, and a coin pearl on a head pin (**photo c**). Make eight.
[4] String a coin pearl on a head pin (**photo d**). Make seven.
[5] Stack a 4mm pearl and a cloisonné bead on a head pin (**photo e**). Make seven.
[6] Stack a 4mm bicone and a cloisonné bead on a head pin (**photo f**). Make six.
[7] String an 8mm fire-polished bead on a head pin. Make six (**photo g**).
[8] Make a wrapped loop (Basics, p. 8) above the top bead on each dangle component. Trim the excess wire and file any sharp edges as necessary.

Necklace assembly

[1] Cut a 22-in. (56cm) piece of flexible beading wire (Basics). String a crimp bead and a 4mm fire-polished bead Go through the loop on a lobster claw clasp and back through the 4mm bead and the crimp bead. Crimp the crimp bead (Basics and **photo h**).
[2] String a 2mm silver bead, a spacer, a rondelle, a 4mm pearl, an 8mm pearl, an 8mm fire-polished bead, and a stick pearl (**photo i**).
[3] String 16 in. (41cm) of pearls, crystals, and beads, adding dangles between them as desired. While there is no set pattern in this necklace, the elements are spaced evenly, with the stick pearls strung about every inch (2.5cm).
[4] Mirror the start of the necklace by stringing a stick pearl, an 8mm fire-polished bead, an 8mm pearl, a 4mm pearl, a rondelle, a spacer, and a 2mm silver bead.

Finishing

[1] String a crimp bead and a 4mm fire-polished bead. Go through the end link of the chain. Go through the 4mm bead and the crimp bead, and pull the wire gently to tighten. Crimp the crimp bead, and trim the tail.
[2] To add the two dangles at the end of the chain, stack an 8mm pearl and a rondelle on a head pin. Stack a 4mm pearl, two spacers, and an 8mm fire-polished bead on a head pin. Make the first half of a wrapped loop on each, attach the dangles to the last chain link, and finish the wraps (**photo j**).

EDITOR'S NOTE:
Christine uses the large opening on her crimping pliers to compress the cut-wire ends on her wrapped loops, making filing the sharp edges unnecessary.

a

b

c

d

e

f

g

h

i

j

Butterfly necklace

This simple multi-strand necklace is designed to show off two artist beads suspended between gold-filled wire swirls and five strands of stones and pearls.

by **Alice Korach**

SUPPLY NOTE:
The two large-hole artist's beads featured here are a lime green "lava bead" and a long ovoid with clear dragonflies over a dichroic core of greens and golds, both by Alethia Donathan, dacsbeads.com.

MATERIALS

necklace 23 in. (58cm)

- 2 art-glass or other large-hole beads, **1 small** (approx. 15–20mm), **1 large** (approx. 30–40mm)
- **1–2 16-in.** (41cm) strands 5–8mm gemstone beads in each of **3 types** (approx. 53 in./1.4m in total length)
- **16-in.** (41cm) strand 6–12mm pearls in each of **2 types**
- 200–300 seed beads, size 11º
- gold-filled clasp
- 2 cones, 18mm with 12mm bottom opening
- 25–30 in. (64–76cm) 18-gauge wire, half hard
- 10 in. (25cm) 20-gauge wire, half hard
- 13 crimp beads
- flexible beading wire, .012–.014
- chainnose pliers
- clamps or tape
- crimping pliers (optional)
- roundnose pliers
- wire cutters

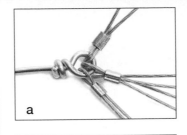

a

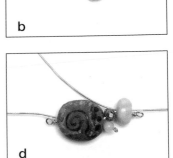

b

c

d

e

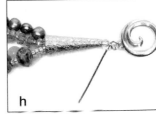

f

g

h

step*by*step

Beaded strands

[1] Cut 3 in. (7.6cm) of 20-gauge wire. Make a wrapped loop (Basics, p. 8). Repeat.

[2] Cut five 16-in. (41cm) pieces of flexible beading wire. Align the ends of two pieces of beading wire. Over both ends, string a crimp bead and one of the loops made in step 1. Go back through the crimp bead, and crimp it (Basics). Working with the same wrapped loop, repeat with another pair of beading wires. Repeat again with the single remaining piece of beading wire (**photo a**).

[3] Working with one strand at a time, string a different type of gemstone or pearl bead on each strand, spacing the beads as desired with 11º seed beads. Make each strand of beads the same length, stopping about 2 in. (5cm) from the end of the wire. End the stone strands with a crimp, a stone, and an 11º. End the pearl strands with a crimp. Braid the strands, and tape or clamp the wires to hold the beads.

[4] Cut three 10-in. (25cm) pieces of beading wire. Crimp them, as in step 2, to the remaining wrapped loop from step 1. String each strand as in step 3, but don't braid them. Tape or clamp the ends.

Butterfly

[1] Cut the 18-gauge wire into four pieces: one 4-in. (10cm) piece; one 5-in. (13cm) piece; one 7-in. (18cm) piece; and one 9-in. (23cm) piece.

[2] Make a medium-to-large wrapped loop at one end of the 5-in. (13cm) wire, and string the small art-glass bead (**photo b**).

[3] Make a small plain loop (Basics) at one end of the 4-in. (10cm) wire, string a small stone bead, go through the large art-glass bead, and make a medium-to-large wrapped loop (**photo c**).

[4] Feed the 9-in. (23cm) wire through the large art-glass bead (you may need to push the small stone bead out of the way so the wire can get through the hole), string an 8mm stone bead, and go through the small art-glass bead (**photo d**). More wire should exit the small art-glass bead than the large art-glass bead.

[5] Feed the 7-in. (18cm) wire through the small art-glass bead (**photo e**).

[6] Using roundnose pliers, make a small bend at the end of one of the wires. Grasp the bend with chainnose pliers, and curve the wire to make a loose spiral. Repeat with the other four wire ends that extend from the art-glass beads as shown in the figure. Position the spirals on top of the wrapped loops and spacer beads (**photo f**).

[7] To keep the spirals in place, cut a 2-in. (5cm) piece of 20-gauge wire, and wrap it around all the wires on one side of the round art-glass bead (**photo g**). Trim the ends, and repeat on the other side of the small art-glass bead.

Assembly

[1] Remove the tape or clamp from one strand of the five-strand section. Pass the beading wire through the loop next to the small art-glass bead and back through several beads at the end of the strand, including the crimp bead. Snug up the beads, and crimp the crimp bead. Repeat with the remaining wire ends, attaching each strand of the five-strand section next to the small art-glass bead and each strand of the three-strand section next to the large art-glass bead.

[2] String a cone on the wire at one end of the necklace. String a small stone bead above the cone, and make the first half of a wrapped loop. Attach one half of the clasp to the loop (**photo h**), and complete the wraps.

SUPPLY NOTE:
The necklace on the left features a focal bead by Dan Eister, daneister.etsy.com; the wood rabbit bead, at right, is imported from China.

Tassel necklace

This tasseled piece spotlights an art bead in a multistrand design and is a great way to use up leftover beads. Best of all, it's a cinch to make.

designed by **Juana Jelen**

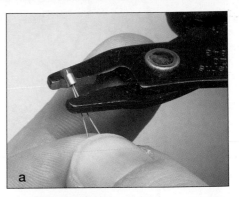

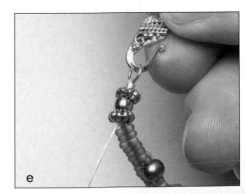

step*by*step

[1] Cut six 24-in. (61cm) pieces of .010 flexible beading wire (Basics, p. 8). This size beading wire kinks easily, so be careful not to run it along a sharp edge.
[2] On one wire, string an 11º seed bead and a crimp bead 2 in. (5cm) from the end. Pass the end back through the crimp and crimp it (Basics and **photo a**).
[3] String one of the larger accent beads, and slide it over the wire tail so it is next to the crimp. String a few seed beads and another accent bead. Repeat until you

have strung 1½–2 in. (3.8–5cm) of beads, completely covering the wire tail.
[4] Repeat steps 2–3 with the other five pieces of wire.
[5] Over all six strands, string a crimp bead. Make sure the beads on all the strands are snug, and crimp the crimp bead **(photo b)**.
[6] String the small large-hole focal bead and the large large-hole focal bead over the crimp **(photo c)**. If desired, place a large spacer bead between the two beads as in the green necklace at left.
[7] String 11½ in. (29.2cm) of 11ºs and accent beads on one of the strands. Clamp or tape the end. Repeat with the remaining five wires, spacing the accent beads as desired **(photo d)**.
[8] Separate the strands into two groups of three strands each.
[9] Over one group of three strands, string a spacer bead, a 4–6mm round bead, a spacer, a crimp bead, and one half of a clasp. Go back through the crimp, spacers, and round bead **(photo e)**. Tighten the strands so the beads are snug, and crimp the crimp bead. Trim the excess wire close to the beads.
[10] Repeat step 9 with the other three strands to attach the other half of the clasp.

MATERIALS
necklace 22 in. (56cm)
- 2 large-hole focal beads, 1 large and 1 small
- 100–120 assorted 2–10mm accent beads
- 2 4–6mm round beads
- hank 11º seed beads
- 10mm spacer bead (optional)
- 4 4–6mm spacer beads
- clasp
- 9 crimp beads
- flexible beading wire, .010
- clamps or tape
- crimping pliers
- wire cutters

Quick change pendant

There are certain pieces of jewelry that are simply an asset to any wardrobe. This easy pendant is designed to slip on and off a chain, leather, or cord necklace, depending on what you plan to wear.

designed by **Beth Stone**

a

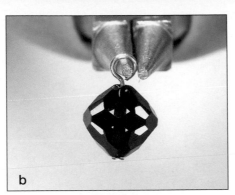

b

c

d

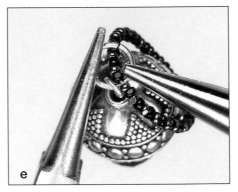

e

step*by*step

[1] Cut a 5-in. (13cm) piece of beading wire (Basics, p. 8). String an alternating pattern of color A and color B 11º seed beads until you have 1¾ in. (4.4cm) of beads. String a crimp bead on one end, and cross the other end of the wire through it (photo a). Crimp the crimp bead. Trim the wire close to the crimp and set aside.

[2] To make a head pin dangle, string an 8–10mm bead on a head pin, and make a plain loop (Basics) above the bead (photo b).

[3] Cut a piece of wire ¾ in. (1.9cm) longer than the bead you'll use for the upper component. Make a plain loop at one end of the wire. String the 15mm bead, and make another plain loop (photo c).

[4] Open the loop on the head pin dangle (Basics), and connect it to the bottom loop of the upper component made in step 3 (photo d). Close the loop.

[5] Open a jump ring (Basics), and connect the top loop of the upper component to the seed bead loop (photo e). Close the jump ring.

MATERIALS

pendant 1½ in. (3.8cm)

- 15mm bead
- 8–10mm bead
- 1g seed beads, size 11º, in each of 2 colors: A, B
- 2½ in. (64mm) 20-gauge wire
- 2-in. (5cm) head pin
- 5mm jump ring
- crimp bead
- flexible beading wire, .012–.014
- crimping pliers
- chainnose pliers
- roundnose pliers
- wire cutters

DESIGN NOTE:

To simplify further, you can make your entire pendant from combination of beads on a head pin, rather than a large bead with a dangle, as in the center pendant (opposite). For this option, follow step 1, then string your combination of beads on a head pin, and make a plain loop. Finish with step 5.

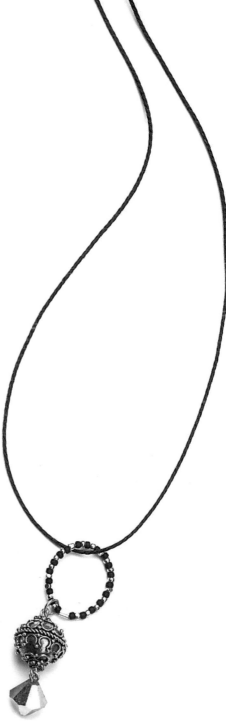

CHAPTER 2
bracelets

Beachy bracelet

Shell buttons help create the perfect summertime accessory. Pearl or crystal dangles accent the shells' gleam with a little glitz of their own.

designed by **Julie Walker**

MATERIALS
bracelet 7 in. (18cm)
- Shellz two-hole buttons (blumenthallansing.com for store list)
  14 square
  12 rectangular
- 7 6mm top-drilled pearls or briolettes
- 10 6mm pearls or round fire-polished beads, color A
- 10 6mm cathedral-cut or round fire-polished beads, color B
- 22 4mm bicone crystals
- 2g size 11º seed beads
- 1g size 15º seed beads
- toggle clasp
- French (bullion) wire
- Fireline 10 lb. test
- beading needles, #10 or #11

step*by*step

[1] On a comfortable length of Fireline, attach a stop bead (Basics, p. 8), leaving a 12-in. (30cm) tail.

[2] Pick up a color B cathedral-cut bead, a color A pearl or 6mm fire-polished bead, and a 4mm bicone crystal **(photo a)**. Repeat eight times.

[3] Pick up a B, an A, an 11º seed bead, a 15º seed bead, a ¼-in. (6mm) piece of French (bullion) wire, and the loop half of a toggle clasp. Sew back through the 15º, 11º, and A **(photo b)**, and pull tight to form a loop.

[4] Make a square dangle by picking up a 15º, an 11º, a 15º, a crystal, a 15º, an 11º, one hole each of two square buttons held back-to-back, an 11º, a 15º, a top-drilled pearl or briolette, a 15º, an 11º, the other hole of both buttons, and an 11º. Sew back through the 15º, crystal, 15º, 11º, and 15º **(photo c)**. Sew through the next B and crystal.

[5] Make a rectangular dangle by picking up a 15º, an 11º, one hole each of two back-to-back rectangular shell buttons, an 11º, a 15º, a crystal, a 15º, an 11º, the buttons' other holes, an 11º, and a 15º. Skip the next A, and sew through the following B **(photo d)**.

[6] Make a square dangle, and sew through the next crystal and A.

[7] Make a rectangular dangle, skip the next B, and sew through the next crystal and A.

[8] Repeat steps 4–7 until you reach the end of the bracelet.

[9] Repeat step 4, sewing through the final B. Remove the stop bead.

[10] Pick up an 11º and one to six 15ºs. (The extra 15ºs allow the bar half of the clasp to move freely.)

[11] Pick up a ¼-in. piece of French (bullion) wire and the bar half of the clasp. Sew back through the 15ºs and the 11º **(photo e)**, and pull tight.

[12] Making sure that there aren't any gaps between beads and all of the drops hang correctly, tie a square knot (Basics) with the tails. Sew back through the bracelet with each tail, tie a few half-hitch knots (Basics), and trim.

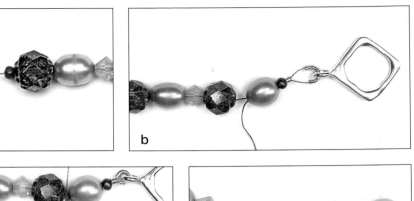

a

b

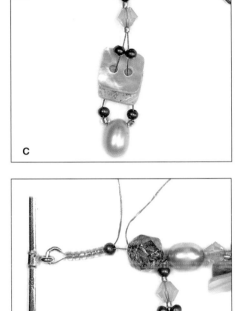

c

d

e

Multistrand twist bracelet

A magnetic clasp is the secret to these easy multistrand bracelets that use up the bits and pieces left over from other jewelry projects. Twist the bracelet before clasping, and the magnetic clasp will hold the twist.

designed by **Irina Miech**

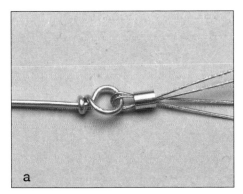

a

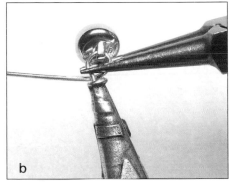

b

MATERIALS
bracelet 7 in. (18cm)
- 12–36 4mm fire-polished Czech crystals
- 10–15g sizes 8º–12º seed beads in a variety of colors
- 12–36 3–4mm flat Bali spacers
- magnetic clasp*
- 2 12mm cones
- 6 in. (15cm) 20-gauge wire, half hard
- 4 crimp beads
- flexible beading wire, .010
- chainnose pliers
- clamps or tape
- crimping pliers (optional)
- roundnose pliers
- wire cutters
- * Note: Pregnant women and people with pacemakers should consult their physicians before wearing magnetic jewelry.

step*by*step

[1] Cut four 21-in. (53cm) pieces of flexible beading wire (Basics, p. 8).

[2] Cut two 3-in. (7.6cm) pieces of wire. On each wire, make a wrapped loop (Basics) small enough to fit inside a cone.

[3] Center two pieces of beading wire in a wrapped loop. Over all four ends, string a crimp bead, sliding the crimp up to the wrapped loop **(photo a)**. Crimp the crimp bead (Basics). Repeat with the other wrapped loop and two pieces of beading wire. Each loop now has four 10½-in. (27cm) lengths of wire coming from it.

[4] String a mix of seed beads, crystals, and spacers on each of the eight wires. Clamp or tape each one when you finish stringing it to keep the beads in place. Make each the length of your wrist circumference.

[5] Remove the tape or clamps from one group of four wires. String a crimp over the four wire ends. Take the ends through the wrapped loop holding the other set of strands, and go back through the crimp bead. Eliminate any slack, and crimp the crimp bead. Trim the excess wire. Repeat on the other side.

[6] String a cone on one of the wires and make the first half of a wrapped loop. Slide one half of a magnetic clasp into the loop **(photo b)**, and finish the wraps. Repeat at the other end of the bracelet.

Meandering river of beads

Beautiful baguette-cut two-strand
crystal spacers connect lively
rows of bubbling beads.

designed by **Karla Schafer**

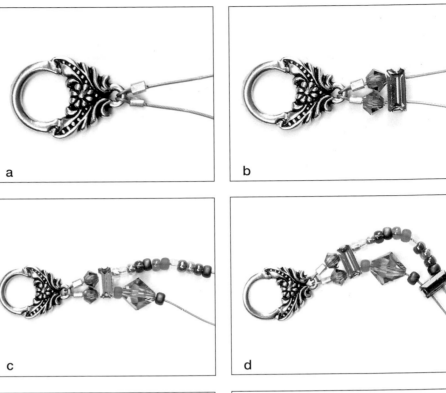

a

b

c

d

e

f

MATERIALS

bracelet 8 in. (20cm)
- 9 8mm bicone crystals
- 6 4mm bicone crystals
- 2g size 8º seed beads
- 10 3 x 7mm baguette 2-hole spacers (Auntie's Beads, auntiesbeads.com)
- clasp
- 4 crimp beads
- flexible beading wire, .014
- crimping pliers
- wire cutters

step*by*step

[1] Cut two 12-in. (30cm) pieces of beading wire (Basics, p. 8). On one end of one wire, string a crimp bead and half of a clasp. Go back through the crimp bead, and crimp it (Basics). Trim the excess wire next to the crimp. Repeat with the second wire on the same clasp half **(photo a)**.

[2] On each wire, string a 4mm bicone crystal. Over both wires, string a two-hole spacer **(photo b)**.

[3] On one wire, string an 8º seed bead, an 8mm bicone crystal, and an 8º. On the other wire, string 12 8ºs **(photo c)**.

[4] Over both wires, string a two-hole spacer **(photo d)**.

[5] Repeat steps 3 and 4, alternating wires **(photo e)**, until you've strung ten two-hole spacers.

[6] On each wire, string a 4mm, an 8º, a 4mm, a crimp bead, and the other half of the clasp. Go back through the crimp bead. Crimp the crimp bead, and trim the excess wire **(photo f)**.

EDITOR'S NOTE:
This design works well with a two-strand clasp as well as a toggle clasp.

Wire-wrapped bracelet

Wrap assorted beads around a sterling silver form to make an upscale accessory in a flash. Make your bracelet with a single layer of beads, or wrap layers upon layers for a sculptural look.

designed by **Miachelle DePiano**

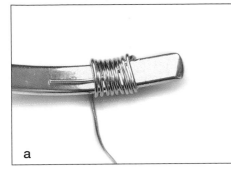

a

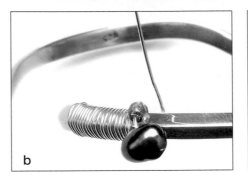

b

c

d

step*by*step

[1] Cut the 24-gauge wire in half. With one piece, make a right-angle bend about ¼–½ in. (6–13mm) from one end.

[2] To create a neat appearance at the ends, wrap the bracelet in two sections, working from each end toward the middle. Place the bent end of the wire along the inside of the bracelet form at one end, pointing the tip of the wire away from the end of the form. Neatly wrap the long end of wire around the form **(photo a)** until the tail is covered.

As you wrap, your wire may kink. To smooth it out, flatten the kinks with nylon-jaw pliers.

[3] Pick up one or two beads, and, holding the beads on the outer surface of the form, wrap the wire around the form **(photo b)**. To anchor the beads, make another wrap **(photo c)**. Repeat until you reach the middle of the bracelet, picking up beads as desired.

[4] To secure the wire, make a few more wraps without any beads. With chainnose pliers, tuck the tail under the beads on top of the bracelet **(photo d)**. Trim, if needed.

[5] Repeat steps 1–4 on the other end of the bracelet.

[6] To make a sculptural bracelet, as in the purple-and-blue bracelet (bottom left), add layers of beads using the following methods:

• Continue wrapping around the bracelet form as before, placing the new beads directly on top of the previous layer. To reduce the amount of exposed wire on the inside of the form, use the previous layer as an armature around which to wrap instead of wrapping around the form.

• If your bead holes will accommodate more than one pass of the wire, string a few beads, and go through a bead on the previous layer.

• String a few beads, go under a wire on a previous layer, do not wrap, and continue.

EDITOR'S NOTE:
Choose a bracelet form with a flat inner surface. Some forms are made with round wire, which makes it difficult to get the beads to stay in place.

MATERIALS
bracelet 6½ in. (16.5cm)
• assorted 4–8mm beads
• 6 ft. (1.8m) 24-gauge wire, dead soft
• bracelet form
  (Metalliferous, metalliferous.com)
• chainnose pliers
• nylon-jaw pliers (optional)
• wire cutters

Wrapped hematite hourglasses

Swirling wire and free-floating seed beads encase hematite hourglass beads. String the bracelet in a simple pattern to emphasize the wire curves.

designed by **Amanda Shero**

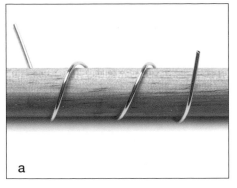

a

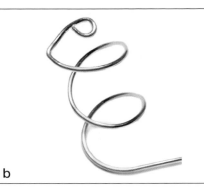

b

c

d

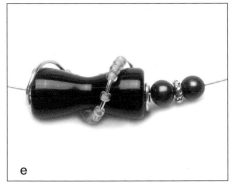

e

step*by*step

Wrapped hourglass bead

[1] Cut 4½ in. (11.4cm) of wire, and, leaving approximately ¾ in. (1.9cm) at each end, wrap it around a ⅜-in. (1cm) dowel twice **(photo a)**.

[2] Slide the wire off the dowel. Make a simple loop at one end of the spiral.

[3] Make a right angle bend approximately ⅛ in. (3mm) from the base of the loop, bending the loop toward the center of the spiral **(photo b)**.

[4] String 20 11º seed beads onto the wire.

[5] Insert an hourglass-shaped bead into the spiral **(photo c)**, centering the wire loop over the bead hole. Line up the bend made in step 3 with the edge of the bead.

[6] Make a right-angle bend in the wire at the opposite end, enclosing the hourglass bead within the spiral, and make a simple loop **(photo d)**.

[7] Adjust the loops to line up with the bead holes.

[8] Repeat steps 1–7 to make a total of five wrapped beads.

Bracelet assembly

[1] Open two 4mm jump rings (Basics, p. 8). Slide them through the loops of one half of a clasp, and close them. Repeat with the other half of the clasp.

[2] Cut 12 in. (30cm) of beading wire (Basics), and secure one end with a clamp or tape. String a wrapped hourglass bead, a 4mm round bead, a spacer bead, and a 4mm **(photo e)**. Repeat three times, then string the last wrapped hourglass bead. Remove the clamp or tape. On each end, string a 4mm and a spacer. Test the fit, and add or remove 4mms to each end as needed.

[3] On one end, string a crimp bead and the jump rings attached to one half of the clasp. Go back through the crimp bead, snug up the loop, and crimp the crimp bead (Basics). Trim the excess wire. Repeat on the other end, leaving a bit of slack to allow the bracelet to curve around your wrist.

MATERIALS

bracelet 8 in. (20cm)
- 5 10 x 20mm hourglass-shaped hematite beads
- 10 4mm round hematite beads
- 100 size 11º seed beads
- 6 6mm silver spacer beads
- toggle clasp
- 22½ in. (57.2cm) 20-gauge wire, dead soft
- 4 4mm inside-diameter (ID) jump rings
- 2 crimp beads
- flexible beading wire, 21 strand, .014
- ⅜-in. (1cm) diameter dowel (2 in./5cm or longer)
- chainnose pliers
- clamp or tape
- crimping pliers
- roundnose pliers
- wire cutters

EDITOR'S NOTE:

Vintage Lucite beads are a great lightweight alternative to the hematite used in the original.

Watch out

Don't be surprised if you keep getting asked for the time while wearing this sparkling watchband. The crystal sections string up so quickly, you'll be able to make one for every outfit and still have time on your hands.

by **Anna Elizabeth Draeger**

a

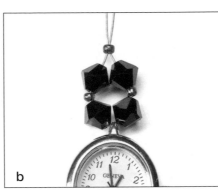

b

c

d

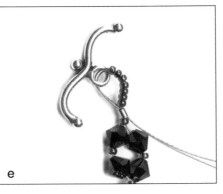

e

f

MATERIALS

watchband 7½–8 in. (19.1–20cm)

- watch face
- 4 10–12mm beads or bicone crystals
- 24 5mm bicone crystals
- 1g size 11º Japanese seed beads
- three-ring toggle clasp
- 8 bead caps
- 2 crimp beads
- flexible beading wire, .012–.014
- clamps or tape
- crimping pliers
- wire cutters

step*by*step

[1] Cut a 12-in. (30cm) piece of flexible beading wire (Basics, p. 8).

[2] Center the watch face on the wire. On each end, string a 5mm bicone crystal, an 11º seed bead, and a 5mm **(photo a)**.

[3] Over both ends, string an 11º **(photo b)**, then string a bead cap, a 10–12mm bead or crystal, a bead cap, and an 11º **(photo c)**.

[4] On each end, string a 5mm, an 11º, and a 5mm **(photo d)**.

[5] Repeat steps 3–4.

[6] Over both ends, string an 11º, and clamp or tape the ends.

[7] Repeat steps 1–6 on the other loop of the watch face.

[8] Remove the clamp or tape from one end of the band. String a crimp bead, seven to nine 11ºs, and one half of a clasp. Go back through the crimp bead, and snug up the beads **(photo e)**. If the loop of the clasp doesn't slide over the 11ºs, remove half the 11ºs, string the clasp, and restring the 11ºs so the clasp is centered. Repeat on the other end.

[9] Adjust the tension of the wires so the 5mms form squares and all the beads are snug. Check the fit. Add or remove beads from each end if necessary.

[10] Crimp the crimp beads (Basics), and trim the excess wire **(photo f)**.

EDITOR'S NOTE:

A toggle clasp with three jump rings for the loop end makes the length of the watchband adjustable. Plus, the rings add weight to the clasp, keeping the watch face on top of your wrist.

Briolette bracelet

Briolettes and crystals combine with silver accent beads for a sparkling bracelet.

designed by **Toni Taylor**

MATERIALS

bracelet 7½ in. (19.1cm)
- 26 5mm cubic zirconia briolettes
- 52 4mm bicone crystals
- 119 2mm seamless sterling silver round beads
- 28 2.1mm sterling silver tube beads
- lobster claw clasp
- 2 4mm soldered jump rings
- 2 4mm jump rings
- Fireline, 6 lb. test
- beading needles, #12
- chainnose pliers

EDITOR'S NOTE:

Do not pull the thread too tight on the first row. A loose tension will allow the crystals to form even clusters when you stitch through the center 2mm beads.

step*by*step

[1] Thread a needle with a comfortable length of Fireline. Leaving a 6-in. (15cm) tail, pick up a 2mm round bead and a soldered jump ring, and sew back through the 2mm (**figure 1, a–b**).

[2] Pick up a tube bead, a 2mm, a crystal, a 2mm, a crystal, and a 2mm (**b–c**). Repeat 12 times (**c–d**).

[3] Pick up a tube, a 2mm, and a soldered jump ring, and sew back through the 2mm (**d–e**).

[4] Pick up a tube, a 2mm, and a crystal. Sew back through the 2mm between the last pair of crystals (**figure 2, a–b**). Pick up a crystal, a 2mm, a tube, a 2mm, and a crystal. Sew through the 2mm between the next pair of crystals (**b–c**). Repeat the pattern to **point d**.

[5] Pick up a crystal, a 2mm, and a tube. Sew through the end 2mm and the jump ring. Sew back through the end 2mm (**d–e**).

[6] Sew through the band to exit at **figure 3, point a**.

[7] Sew diagonally through the first cluster of crystals (**figure 3, a–b**). Pick up a 2mm, a briolette, and a 2mm, and sew through the adjacent crystal and the center 2mm (**b–c**). Retrace the thread path of the briolette embellishment.

[8] Continue diagonally through the next crystal (**c–d**). Add a briolette embellishment to the other edge as in step 7 (**d–e**). Retrace the thread path, and continue through the next crystal, 2mm, tube, and 2mm (**e–f**).

[9] Repeat steps 7 and 8 for the length of the bracelet.

[10] Secure the Fireline with a few half-hitch knots (Basics, p. 8) between beads, and trim.

[11] Open a jump ring (Basics), attach it to the soldered jump ring on one end, and close the ring. Repeat on the other end, but attach a lobster claw clasp before closing the jump ring.

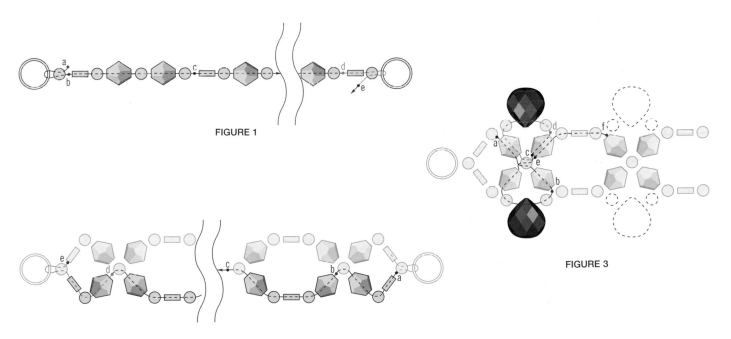

FIGURE 1

FIGURE 2

FIGURE 3

A garden of charms

Combine fun glass beads in the shape of
flowers, leaves, butterflies, and ladybugs
to make an adorable charm bracelet —
not your grandmother's charm bracelet,
but a stretchy colorful multistrand
with plenty of dangles to shimmer
on your wrist.

by **Cheryl Phelan**

MATERIALS

bracelet 7 in. (18cm)

- **30–35** assorted beads for dangles
- assorted **2–6mm** accent beads and crystals
- **3g** size **11º** beads in each of **3** colors
- spacer bar with 5 holes
- **5 ft. (1.6m) 22-gauge** wire (makes 20 top-hole bead dangles)
- **30–35 2-in. (5cm)** head pins
- ribbon elastic
- twisted wire beading needle
- G-S Hypo Cement
- chainnose pliers
- clamps or tape
- roundnose pliers
- wire cutters

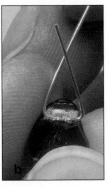

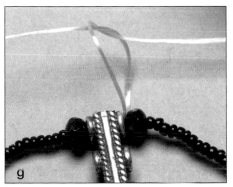

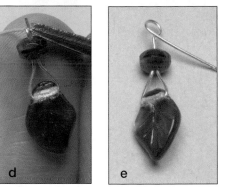

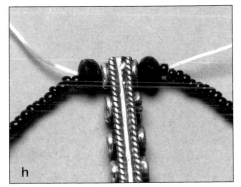

step*by*step

Dangles

[1] On a head pin, string a pleasing arrangement of beads (example: a seed bead, a butterfly, and a crystal).

Make a wrapped loop (Basics, p. 8) above the beads. The loop should be large enough to slide over the seed beads, but smaller than the accent beads. Before completing the wrap, test the size of the loop by stringing an accent bead and a few seed beads on elastic and passing the loop over them **(photo a)**. Each dangle should vary in length from ½–¾ in. (1.3–1.9cm), including the loop. Repeat to make 15–35 head pin dangles. You'll make fewer head pin dangles if you're also going to make leaf dangles.

[2] To make leaf dangles (with beads that have a hole across the top), cut a 3-in. (7.6cm) piece of wire, and string the bead on the wire about ½ in. (1.3cm) from the end. With your fingers, bend both ends of the wire up until they cross above the center of the bead **(photo b)**. Use chainnose pliers to bend both wires slightly so they are parallel above the bead **(photo c)**. Be careful not to crack the bead.

[3] String an accent bead over both wires, and slide it against the bend. Grasp the long wire with chainnose pliers and make a right angle bend about ⅛ in. (3mm)

above the accent bead. Cut the short wire so it is flush with the right angle bend **(photo d)**. Make the first half of a wrapped loop **(photo e)**, then finish the wraps.

[4] Repeat steps 2 and 3 to make 15–20 leaf dangles, if desired.

Bracelet

[1] Cut five 12-in. (30cm) lengths of elastic. Clamp or tape one end of each strand. String a mix of 11º seed beads, dangles, and accent beads on each one. String the dangles over groups of five to 10 11ºs so the dangles slide. Each strand should be about ½ in. longer than your wrist circumference. As you string the strands, lay them in parallel lines to be

sure the dangles are staggered along each strand **(photo f)**.

[2] Remove the clamp or tape from a strand, and string it through the top hole of the spacer bar. Knot the elastic tails together with a square knot (Basics and **photo g**). Keep the elastic relaxed but tight enough so it doesn't show between the beads. Dab the knot with glue, and pull it into a bead. Run the tails through a few more beads in opposite directions **(photo h)**. To keep the tails in place, pull on each tail and glue the elastic where it exits the bead.

[3] After the glue is dry, trim the tail as close to the bead as possible. Repeat with the remaining strands.

earrings

Turning wheel earrings

Textured, hollow copper disk beads put together
with a silver rim and rivet, though fairly large,
are lightweight enough to make beautiful,
comfortable earrings. Make your own earwires
to complement the copper components.

by **Alice Korach**

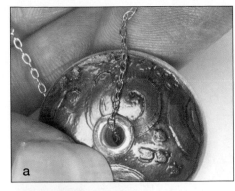

a

b

c

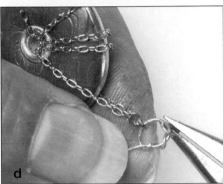

d

e

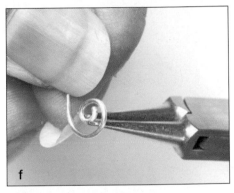

f

g

step*by*step

Wrapping the bead

[1] Cut the chain into two 7⅜-in. (18.7cm) pieces.

[2] Thread one piece through the rivet hole of the disk bead, leaving an end on top that's about ½ in. (1.3cm) longer than the radius of the bead (**photo a**). Then wrap the long end from back to front around the edge and through the hole four times. Keep the wraps next to each other and don't cross the chain over itself as it goes through the hole (**photo b**).

[3] Cut a 2-in. (5cm) length of 24-gauge wire, and thread it through the last link on each end of the chain. With round-nose pliers, make a fairly large ring by crossing the wire tails around one jaw of the pliers (**photo c**). Slide the chain links into the ring. Jiggle the chain wraps until the ends are even and the bead hangs straight.

TEMPLATE

[4] Use chainnose pliers to feed the wire ends through the ring, wrapping it the same way you wrapped the chain around the bead (**photo d**). Make four to six wraps as evenly spaced as possible.

[5] When the end of the wire reaches the chain, make a small, tight wrap next to the chain. Trim the wire tails, and press them in with chainnose pliers (**photo e**). Repeat with the other end of the wire on the other side of the chain.

[6] Repeat to make a second disk-and-chain component.

Earwires

[1] Cut 3 in. (7.6cm) of 20-gauge wire, and shape it following the full-size **template** below. Start by making a small spiral for the hanging loop with roundnose pliers (**photo f**). When the spiral matches the template, shape the curve with your fingers.

[2] File the end that will go into your ear so it's smooth and rounded. If you wish, hammer both sides of the entire earwire on an anvil or steel block to harden and texture it. Then thread the wrapped ring on the wire from the back to the bottom of the spiral (**photo g**).

[3] Make another ear wire to match the first, and attach the second disk-and-chain component.

MATERIALS

one pair earrings

- 2 copper and silver riveted disk beads (Fae Mellichamp, Chimera Glass Works, chimeraglassworks.com)
- 6 in. (15cm) 20-gauge wire, half hard
- 4 in. (10cm) 24-gauge wire, half hard
- 14¾ in. (37.5cm) cable chain, 2.2mm links
- chainnose pliers
- bench block or anvil (optional)
- hammer (optional)
- metal file
- roundnose pliers
- wire cutters

On multiple levels

These dramatic chandelier earrings allow for any number of variations of materials, and all that's required are basic wire-working skills and an adventurous spirit. Use chain to create length and movement; shorten or lengthen the pieces of chain to get different sizes and effects.

designed by **Melody MacDuffee**

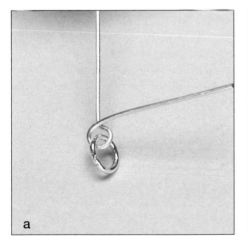

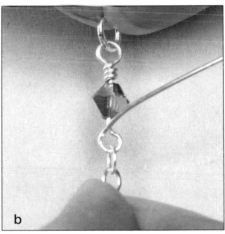

step*by*step

Blue-and-silver earrings
[1] Cut two three-link pieces of 1.25mm chain, two nine-link pieces, and one 11-link piece.
[2] Cut a 2-in. (5cm) piece of 24-gauge wire. Make the first half of a wrapped loop (Basics, p. 8). Attach the loop to a soldered jump ring **(photo a)** and finish the wraps.
[3] String a color A 4mm crystal on the wire against the wrap. Make the first half of a wrapped loop above the crystal and in the same plane as the first loop. Attach the end link of a three-link piece of chain **(photo b)**. Finish the wraps.
[4] Cut a 2-in. (5cm) piece of 24-gauge wire, and make the first half of a wrapped loop. Attach the other end link of the chain from the previous step, and finish the wraps.
[5] String a color B crystal on the wire, and make the first half of a wrapped loop. Attach the end links of a nine-link piece of chain and the 11-link chain **(photo c)**. Complete the wraps.

MATERIALS

blue-and-silver earrings
- bicone crystals
  10 4mm, color A
  14 4mm, color B
  8 4mm, color C
  24 3mm
- 4 in. (10cm) 22-gauge wire
- 16 in. (41cm) 24-gauge wire
- 18 in. (46cm) chain, 1.25mm links
- 28 2-in. (5cm) head pins
- 2 4–6mm soldered jump rings
- pair of post earring findings

fire-polished-and-gold earrings
- 32 4mm Czech fire-polished beads
- 24 3mm bicone crystals
- 4 in. (10cm) 22-gauge wire
- 16 in. (41cm) 24-gauge wire
- 18 in. (46cm) chain, 2.5mm links
- 28 2-in. (5cm) head pins
- pair of earring findings

AB-crystal earrings
- bicone crystals
  12 4mm
  8 6mm
  2 8mm
  4 6 x 12mm
- 4 in. (10cm) 22-gauge wire
- 8 in. (20cm) 24-gauge wire
- 12 in. (30cm) chain, 1.25mm links
- 16 2-in. (5cm) head pins
- 2 4–6mm soldered jump rings
- pair of post earring findings

bone-bead earrings
- 2 10 x 20mm bone beads
- 4mm round beads
  10 turquoise
  12 tiger eye
- 4 in. (10cm) 22-gauge wire
- 8 in. (20cm) 24-gauge wire
- 12 in. (30cm) chain, 1.25mm links
- 14 2-in. (5cm) head pins
- 2 3-to-1 findings
- pair of earring findings

all projects
- chainnose pliers
- roundnose pliers
- wire cutters

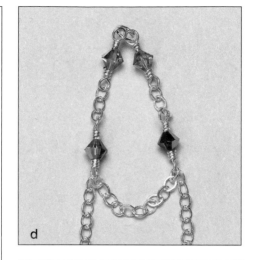

d

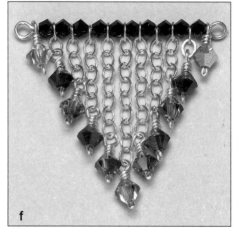

f

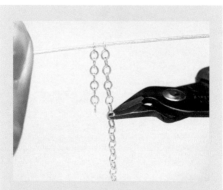

EDITOR'S NOTE:
To cut multiple pieces of chain the same length, cut the first piece to the desired length, slide the end link on a wire, and string the end link of the remaining chain on the wire next to the cut piece. Hold the wire so both chains hang freely and cut the second piece to match the first.

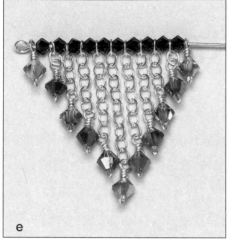

e

[6] Repeat steps 2–5, attaching the remaining chains from step 1 to the same soldered jump ring and the other end of the 11-link chain (the "crossing chain") **(photo d)**. Make sure the crossing chain is not twisted before attaching it to the second side.

[7] On a head pin, string a color A crystal, and make a wrapped loop. Repeat to make another bottom end dangle.

[8] For the rest of the bottom dangles, work as in step 7, but attach a length of chain before completing the wraps. The crystal colors will alternate and the chain lengths will differ as specified below:
- Color B crystal, two chain links (make two)
- Color C crystal, four chain links (make two)
- Color B crystal, six chain links (make two)
- Color C crystal, eight chain links (make two)
- Color A crystal, ten chain links (make one)

[9] For the crossbar, cut a 2-in. piece of 22-gauge wire, and make a simple loop at one end.

[10] Starting with an bottom end dangle, string one dangle from each set in graduated order, placing a 3mm crystal between each dangle. String the remaining dangles as a mirror image of the first half **(photo e)**.

[11] Trim the wire to ⅜ in. (1cm) past the last dangle, and make a simple loop in the same plane as the first **(photo f)**.

[12] Open a loop on the crossbar, attach an end link of chain from step 6 (photo g), and close the loops tightly.
[13] String a color B crystal on a head pin and make the first half of a wrapped loop. Repeat twice, using a 3mm for each dangle. Slide the loop of the color B dangle through the middle link of the crossing chain (photo h), and finish the wraps. Skip a link, and attach a 3mm dangle on each side of the center dangle.
[14] Open the loop of an earring finding, and attach it to the soldered jump ring.
[15] Make a second earring to match the first.

Fire-polished-and-gold earrings

The fire-polished bead earrings follow the same basic instructions as the blue and silver earrings, but use chain with larger links (2.5mm) and one color of fire-polished beads instead of three colors of 4mm crystals. Follow the instructions above, with the following changes:

In step 1, cut two two-link pieces, two seven-link pieces, and one nine link piece of chain. Where the instructions above call for the three-link chain, use the two-link chain, and substitute the seven- and nine-link chains for the nine- and eleven-link chains.

In step 8, use the following pattern to make the dangles with the 2.5mm chain:
• bead, one link (make two)
• bead, two links (make two)
• bead, three links (make two)
• bead, four links (make two)
• bead, five links (make one)

In step 13, don't skip links when attaching dangles to the long linking chain.

AB-crystal earrings

[1] Cut three 13-link and one 27-link pieces of chain.
[2] Follow step 2 for the blue-and-silver earrings. String a 4mm crystal, and make the first half of a wrapped loop. Attach the end link of two 13-link pieces of chain, and finish the wraps.
[3] Make another crystal unit, and attach one loop to the jump ring. Attach the other loop to the remaining 13-link chain and the end link on the closest

g

chain from the previous step (the crossing chain). Don't twist the crossing chain.
[4] Cut a 2-in. piece of 22-gauge wire and make a simple loop at one end. Slide an end link of the 27-link chain on the wire and string a 6 x 12mm crystal, a 6mm crystal, and a 6 x 12mm. Go through the other end link on the long chain, and make another loop in the same plane as the first.
[5] On a head pin, string an 8mm crystal and make the first half of a wrapped loop. Attach the loop to the middle link of the 27-link chain and finish the wrap. Repeat to add the following crystal dangles to each side of the 8mm:
• skip three links; attach a 6mm crystal dangle
• skip a link; attach a 4mm crystal dangle
• skip a link; attach a 4mm crystal dangle
[6] Make a 6mm dangle, and hang it from the middle link of the crossing chain.
[7] Attach the earring finding.
[8] Make a second earring to match the first.

Bone-bead earrings

Follow the instructions for the AB-crystal earrings with the changes listed below, and refer to the picture of the bone earring to determine the placement of each bead color.

In steps 2 and 3, the bead units are attached to the end loops on the finding instead of to a jump ring.

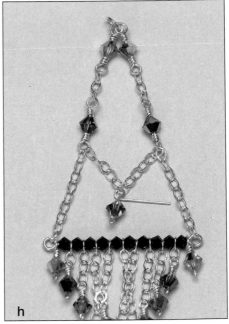

h

In step 4, attach the chain between the middle and end beads. The length of the middle bead will determine the length of chain (this one has 23 links).

In step 5, make five bead dangles and attach the first one to the middle link of chain. Add two dangles to each side: skip one link, add a dangle, skip two links, and add a dangle.

In step 7, attach a dangle to the middle loop on the finding.

Feathered finery

Anglers beware! Beaders are raiding your fishing
supplies. Fly-tying trimmings come in an amazing
assortment of feathers — every color, every size —
from the sleek to the fluffy. Opulent, sable marabou
feathers are a wonderful inspiration for jewelry designs
and fun plumage to add to any wardrobe.

designed by **Pam O'Connor**

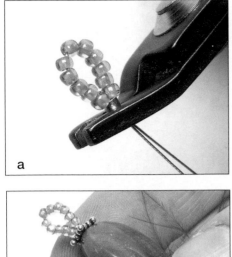

a

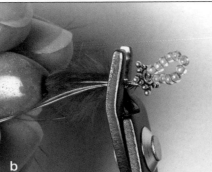

b

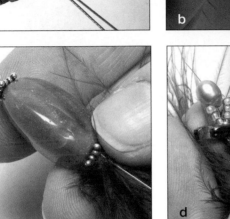

c

d

MATERIALS

one pair earrings
- 2 15 x 12mm stone beads with large holes
- 4 6 x 4mm top-drilled, drop-shaped pearls
- 106 size 11º seed beads
- 4 sterling silver spacer beads
- 8 crimp beads
- pair of earring findings
- flexible beading wire, .014
- 2 marabou feathers
- chainnose pliers
- crimping pliers
- wire cutters

SUPPLY NOTES:
- Marabou feathers are sold sewn together in a row. Choose two that have nice symmetrical shapes and cut the threads to release them.
- Be sure your stone bead and silver spacers have large enough holes to slide easily over a crimped crimp bead (approximately 2mm).

step*by*step

[1] Measure each feather from the tip and cut it (from the shaft end) to 3½ in. (8.9cm) in length.

[2] Cut an 8-in. (40cm) piece of flexible beading wire (Basics, p. 8), and center 11 11º seed beads on it.

[3] Thread both wire ends through a crimp bead. Tighten the bead loop so it is snug, and crimp the crimp (Basics and **photo a**). String a silver spacer over the crimp bead, then string a second crimp bead over both wire ends.

[4] String a spacer bead and the stone bead onto the cut end of the feather so that ½ in. (1.3cm) of the feather protrudes from the stone bead.

[5] Insert the feather's cut end into the second crimp bead so that ¼ in. (6mm) emerges out the top. Crimp the crimp bead around the feather and wire ends **(photo b)**.

[6] Put the two wire ends through the stone bead and spacer bead on the feather. Slide the stone bead and spacer bead up so they are snug against the other spacer bead and beaded loop **(photo c)**.

[7] Arrange the wire ends so they both lie on the same side of the feather. String 20 11ºs, a crimp, three 11ºs, a pearl, and three 11ºs onto one wire.

[8] Insert the wire end back through the crimp and a few more beads. Tighten so that the beads are snug against the silver spacer and around the pearl. Crimp the crimp **(photo d)** and trim the wire.

[9] String 10 11ºs, a crimp, three 11ºs, a pearl, and three 11ºs on the other wire.

[10] Repeat step 8.

[11] Use chainnose pliers to open the loop (Basics) on the earring wire and insert the beaded loop. Close the wire loop.

[12] Make a second earring to match the first.

Gem-set pearls

by **Louise Malcolm**

These teardrop coin pearls are matched in pairs and set on both sides with a variety of tiny, faceted stones in gold bezels. The pearls work as either plain earrings or in fancier versions with briolette drops suspended from chains below them.

step*by*step

Earrings with dangles

[1] To make a dangle, cut a 2-in. (5cm) piece of 24-gauge wire. Center a briolette on the wire, and cross the wire tails, making a circular loop above the briolette **(photo a)**. Using chainnose pliers, bend one wire straight above the briolette, forming the shaft **(photo b)**. Make a right-angle bend above the pliers **(photo c)**. Using roundnose pliers, make the first half of a wrapped loop (Basics, p. 8). Where the tail of the wire will cross the shaft, bend the tail straight down, parallel to the shaft **(photo d)**. Make five dangles.

[2] Cut five pieces of chain to the following lengths: three links, five links, seven links, nine links, and 11 links. Slide an end link of each chain into the loop of a dangle **(photo e)**.

[3] Position the chainnose pliers across the briolette loop. Wrap the unused tail around both vertical wires. Continue wrapping until you reach the top loop **(photo f)**. Trim both tails.

[4] Cut a 3-in. (7.6cm) piece of 24-gauge wire, and make the first half of a plain loop or a wrapped loop (Basics). String the end links of all five dangles onto the loop **(photo g)**, and complete the wraps.

[5] String the pearl, pointed-end up, and make a wrapped loop above it. Open an earring finding (Basics), string the pearl on the loop, and close the loop.

[6] Make a second earring as a mirror image of the first.

Plain earrings

String a gem-set pearl on a head pin, and make a wrapped loop. Open an earring wire, attach the wrapped loop **(photo h)**, and close the earring wire.

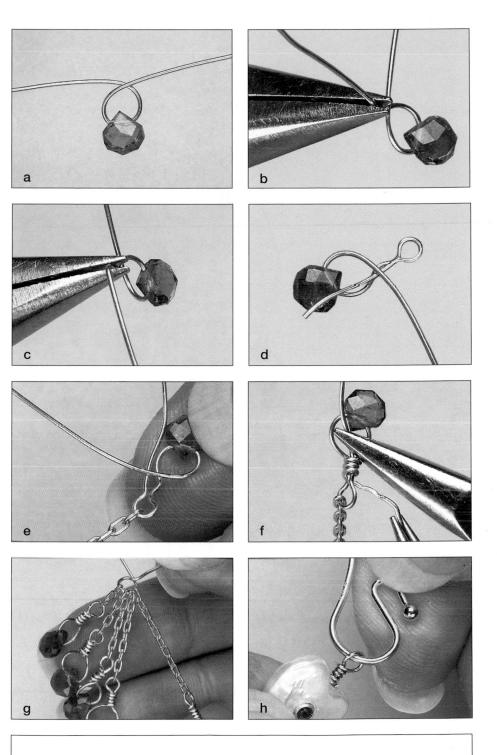

MATERIALS

both pairs of earrings
- 2 teardrop coin pearls with inset gems (Opal Illusions, opalillusions.com)
- pair of earring findings
- chainnose pliers
- roundnose pliers
- wire cutters

earrings with dangles
- 10 5–8mm gemstone briolettes
- 30 in. (76cm) 24-gauge wire, half hard
- 6 in. (15cm) cable chain, 2.2mm links
- 2 2-in. (5cm) head pins

In one ear...

Personalize metal earrings and frame your face with a favorite phrase, quote, rhyme, or lyric accented by a variety of beaded dangles. Let your chosen beads guide you, as the tiny shells did for the project's designers, or choose your words first, and then have fun finding the perfect beads to enhance your theme.

designed by **Janice Berkebile** *and* **Tracy Stanley**

a

b

c

MATERIALS

one pair of earrings

- 8–15 3–6mm crystals, in various shapes and colors
- 4–8 small shell beads
- 2–6 4mm sew-on crystal sequins or flat spacers
- 2 26-gauge sterling silver teardrop-shaped blanks (Rio Grande, riogrande.com)
- 6 in. (15cm) 20-gauge sterling silver wire, half hard
- 12 2-in. (5cm) sterling silver decorative head pins
- bench block
- chainnose pliers
- chasing hammer
- cup bur or small files
- liver of sulfur/patination liquid (optional)
- metal hole punch (Contenti, contenti.com)
- metal decorative stamps (optional) (Beaducation, beaducation.com)
- 1/16–1/8-in. (2–3mm) metal letter stamps (Contenti)
- paintbrush (optional)
- polishing cloth (optional)
- roundnose pliers
- tape
- utility hammer
- wire cutters

step*by*step

Earring base

[1] Using a hole punch, make five holes at the bottom of a silver blank, at least ⅛ in. (3mm) from the edge and ⅛ in. (3mm) apart. Make a hole at the top for an earring finding and a hole near the center for a surface decoration **(photo a)**.

[2] Tape the blank to a bench block. Assemble the letter stamps that spell out one half of your chosen phrase. Carefully place each stamp, checking that the letter is oriented correctly. Hold the stamp steady. With a utility hammer, give the stamp one solid and heavy tap, as if you're hammering a nail **(photo b)**. More than one hit may cause the stamp to bounce, creating a blurry shadow image.

[3] After you've spelled your word or phrase, use design stamps to decorate some of the background. Use the same singular, firm hammer hit as you did for the letter stamps.

[4] If the blank is warped from stamping, flatten it by lightly hammering the back with the large, flat side of a chasing hammer.

[5] Using the small rounded side of the chasing hammer, gently hammer around the entire front edge of the blank, creating a dimpled edge **(photo c)**.

SUPPLY NOTE:

Sterling silver blanks are easy to find in many shapes and sizes — no saw or metal shears required. Most don't have holes where you'd like them, but you can use an inexpensive metal hole punch to make consistent holes quickly and cleanly.

Flatten the blank again if necessary.

[6] Repeat steps 1–5 to make another base, stamping it with the other half of your chosen phrase.

Dangles

[1] On a decorative head pin, string a bicone crystal and the open end of a shell bead. Gently manipulate the wire until the crystal partially tucks inside the shell. Make the first half of a wrapped

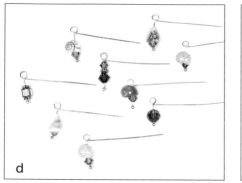

d

e

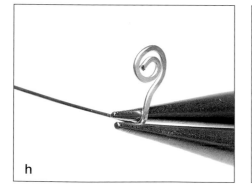

f

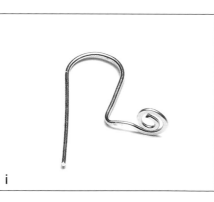

g

h

i

j

k

loop (Basics, p. 8). (Some shells are delicate, so take care while wrapping.) Repeat to make five dangles for each base, combining shells, crystals, silver spacers, and sequins as desired (photo d).

[2] Slide the loop of a dangle into a hole at the bottom of a base. Finish the wrapped loop, coiling the wraps over the top of the crystal or shell. Or, to make a wrapped loop with a spiral embellishment, use roundnose pliers to make a tiny bend at the tip of the wire. With chainnose pliers, grip the bent end, and tightly curl it to create a small spiral (photo e). Complete the wrapped loop, coiling the wraps over the top of the crystal or shell and carefully bending the wire to position the spiral in front (photo f).

[3] Attach the remaining nine dangles to the bases, coiling over the top beads and making spiral embellishments as desired.

Earring finding

[1] Cut a 3-in. (7.6cm) piece of 20-gauge wire. Make a small spiral at the end of the wire. Using the large, flat side of your chasing hammer, lightly hammer the spiral (photo g).

[2] Using roundnose pliers, make a small right-angle bend below the spiral (photo h). This initial, incomplete bend will keep the spiral out of the way so you can easily hammer the front of the earring finding.

[3] Using the large end of your round-nose pliers, make a rounded bend in the opposite direction of the last bend (photo i). Lightly hammer in front of the bend you just made without flattening the rounded portion that will go through the ear.

[4] Use roundnose pliers to slightly bend the tip of the wire up. Trim the wire to the desired length, and round off any sharp edges with a cup bur or small files.

[5] Repeat steps 1–4 to make a second

earring finding, forming the spiral in the opposite direction to mirror the first.

Finishing

[1] To make the surface decoration, string a sequin or flat spacer on a decorative head pin. String the head pin through the central hole of a base, front to back. With roundnose pliers, bend the head pin at a right angle very close to the base.

[2] Use roundnose pliers to grip the wire at the bend. Wrap the wire once around one tip of the pliers (photo j). Keep gripping and wrapping the wire until you've created a spiral large enough to hold the sequin or spacer securely to the base. The sequin or spacer should be able to spin, but if the connection's too loose, gently grip the ball of the head pin and bend it slightly to tighten it.

[3] Slide the earring onto an earring finding. Grip the bottom of the earring finding's spiral with roundnose pliers. Bend the spiral up (photo k) until the earring is secured on the wire and able to swing freely.

[4] If you're using pearls or any delicate stones, carefully brush liver of sulfur or another type of patination liquid on only the metal portion of the earring, if desired. If your dangles are all crystals or nonstainable beads, you can dip the entire earring into the liquid. Once the earring is darkened, rinse and dry it.

[5] Use a polishing cloth to lightly rub off some of the patina, bringing out the details and texture.

[6] Repeat steps 1–5 to finish a second earring.

EDITOR'S NOTE:
Make keepsake jewelry by stamping your children's (or grandchildren's) names on silver blanks. Use crystals in their birthstone colors to make dangles, and attach the dangles to the blanks.

Crisscross earrings

Gold-filled and sterling small-link chains give dangle earrings a delicate look.

designed by **Melody MacDuffee**

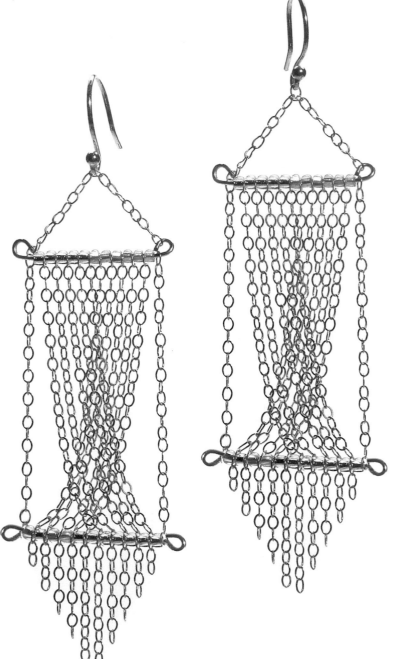

step*by*step

[1] Cut two 2½-in. (6.4cm) pieces of 22-gauge wire, and straighten each piece. On one end of each, place an earring back or wrap with tape.

[2] Cut five 26-link pieces of both sterling and gold-filled chain.

[3] Cut both sterling and gold-filled chain in the following lengths: 25 links, 11 links, nine links, seven links, five links, and three links **(photo a)**.

[4] Cut a 17-link piece of chain in either gold-filled or sterling to match the earring findings. String an earring finding through the center link of the 17-link chain **(photo b)**.

[5] On one piece of wire, string one end of the 17-link chain, the 25-link sterling chain, and a gold-lined 11º seed bead.

String a 26-link sterling chain and a gold-lined 11º. Repeat four times.

String a 26-link gold-filled chain and a silver-lined 11º. Repeat four times.

String the 25-link gold-filled chain and the other end of the 17-link chain **(photo c)**.

Secure the wire end with tape or an earring back.

[6] On the second wire, string the other end link of the 25-link sterling chain and a silver-lined 11º.

String the first 26-link gold-filled chain, the three-link sterling chain, and a silver-lined 11º.

String the second 26-link gold-filled chain, the five-link sterling chain, and a silver-lined 11º.

String the third 26-link gold-filled chain, the seven-link sterling chain, and a silver-lined 11º.

String the fourth 26-link gold-filled chain, the nine-link sterling chain, and a silver-lined 11º.

String the fifth 26-link gold-filled chain, the 11-link sterling chain, and a silver-lined 11º **(photo d)**.

[7] Crossing the sterling 26-link chains behind the gold-filled chains, string the first 26-link sterling chain, the 11-link gold-filled chain, and a gold-lined 11º.

String the second 26-link sterling chain, the nine-link gold-filled chain, and a gold-lined 11º.

String the third 26-link sterling chain, the seven-link gold-filled chain,

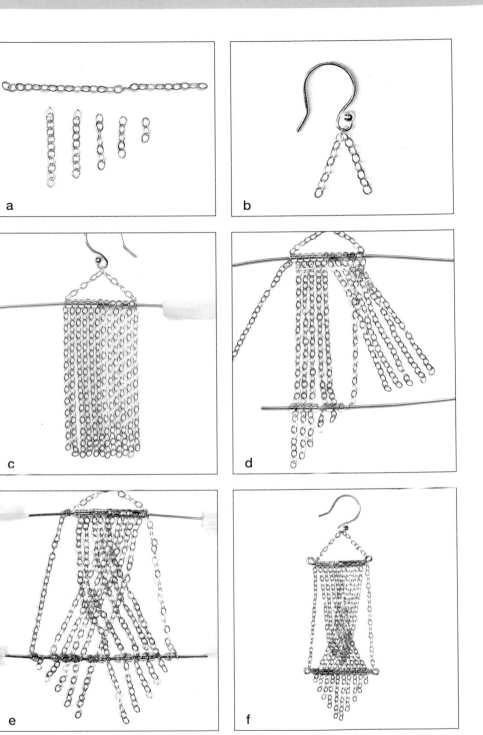

a

b

c

d

e

f

and a gold-lined 11º.

String the fourth 26-link sterling chain, the five-link gold-filled chain, and a gold-lined 11º.

String the fifth 26-link sterling chain, the three-link gold-filled chain, and a gold-lined 11º.

String the 25-link gold-filled chain **(photo e)**.

[8] Remove the earring backs or tape from the wires. Make a simple loop on each end of both wires so the tail

touches the wire **(photo f)**. Position the earring-wire chain in the top loops.

[9] Make a second earring to match the first.

Chained beads

DESIGN VARIATION
Instead of using wire to hang
the two beads from the two
chain pieces, use head pins and
omit the chain loop between the
beads (as in the rock crystal and
silver earrings, second from left).

These simple but stylish earrings are a good way to use up leftover beads and chain — the design uses only six beads and a few inches of chain. Try adapting the design to flatter different outfits: pearls and thin gold chain for dressy occasions, malachite and chunky rollo chain for jeans, and Bali granulated silver beads with the heaviest chain to go from day to evening.

by **Louise Malcolm**

MATERIALS
one pair earrings
• 6 6–12mm beads
• 12 in. (30cm) 24-gauge wire
• 4–6 in. (10–15cm) chain
• pair of earring findings
• chainnose pliers
• roundnose pliers
• wire cutters

step*by*step

[1] Cut two ⅝-in. (1.6cm) and two ⅜-in. (1cm) pieces of chain. Cut six 2-in. (5cm) pieces of wire.
[2] Make a wrapped loop on the end of one wire (Basics, p. 8). String a 6–12mm bead, and make the first half of another wrapped loop.
[3] Pull the end link of a ⅝-in. and a ⅜-in. chain into the loop (photo a), then finish the wraps.
[4] Make the first half of a wrapped loop on a piece of wire from step 1. Slide the end link of one of the chains from step 3 into the loop and finish the wraps. Repeat with another piece of wire and chain (photo b).
[5] String a bead on one of the wires and make the first half of a wrapped loop. String a bead on the other wire, and make the first half of a wrapped loop. Slide an end link of the remaining chain into one of the loops, and finish the wraps (photo c).
[6] Experiment with the length you want the bottom chain loop to be (photo d — this one is about 1 in./2.5cm) and cut off the excess chain. Pull the end link into the other unwrapped loop, and finish the wraps.
[7] Open the loop on an earring finding (Basics), attach the top bead's loop, and close the loop.
[8] Make a second earring to match the first.

a

b

c

d

107

Boho hoops

Create graceful earrings that are both stylish and retro, and a breeze to make! Suspend a shimmering mother-of-pearl bead in generous double hoops for earrings with a Bohemian vibe.

designed by **Zurina Ketola**

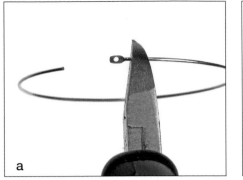

a

b

c

d

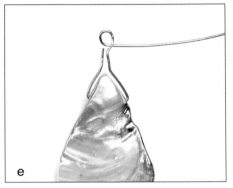

e

f

g

MATERIALS
one pair earrings
- 2 ¾ x 1-in. (1.9 x 2.5cm) top-drilled fan- or teardrop-shaped mother-of-pearl beads (Fire Mountain Gems, firemountaingems.com)
- 4g Japanese cylinder beads
- 2 2½-in. (6.4cm) sterling silver endless hoop earrings (artbeads.com)
- 2 2-in. (5cm) sterling silver endless hoop earrings (artbeads.com)
- 8 in. (20cm) 22-gauge wire, half hard
- 2 5mm jump rings
- 2 2mm jump rings
- pair of earring findings
- chainnose pliers
- roundnose pliers
- wire cutters

step*by*step

[1] Cut the eye off of a 2-in. (5cm) hoop earring **(photo a)**, and make a plain loop (Basics, p. 8) at one end.
[2] String cylinder beads on the hoop, leaving ¼ in. (6mm) of wire at the end. Make another loop **(photo b)**.
[3] Repeat steps 1 and 2 with a 2½-in. (6.4cm) hoop.
[4] Cut a 4-in. (10cm) piece of wire, and string a mother-of-pearl bead, leaving 1½ in. (3.8cm) of wire on one side of the bead.
[5] Cross the wires above the bead **(photo c)**.
[6] Use chainnose pliers to bend both wires straight up and parallel. Cut the shorter wire to ⅛ in. (3mm) above the bend **(photo d)**.
[7] Make the first half of a wrapped loop (Basics) with the long wire,

keeping the loop in the same plane as the bead **(photo e)**. Make several wraps around both wires **(photo f)**. Trim the excess wire.
[8] Open a 2mm jump ring (Basics), and attach the wrapped loop. Close the jump ring.
[9] Open a 5mm jump ring, and attach a loop of the 2½-in. earring hoop, a loop of the 2-in. earring hoop, the 2mm jump ring, the remaining loop of the 2-in. earring hoop, and the remaining loop of the 2½-in. earring hoop **(photo g)**. Attach the 5mm jump ring to an earring finding. Close the jump ring.
[10] Make a second earring to match the first.

EDITOR'S NOTE:
To make your own earring hoops, shape 22-gauge sterling silver wire around a small bottle or jar.

Creative clusters

If you're looking for ways to get maximum wear from a few basic earring styles, consider this modular approach. Assemble your beads in clusters attached to their own split rings, so you can add or remove them from your earrings as you like. Coordinate the colors for a floral effect, and experiment with other color and bead combinations to build a wardrobe of creative clusters.

by **Mindy Brooks**

a

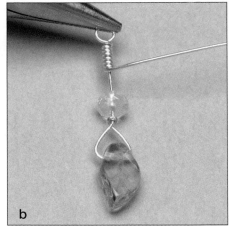

b

c

step*by*step

Leaf clusters

[1] Cut eight 5-in. (13cm) pieces of wire. String a glass leaf ¾ in. (1.9cm) from the end of one wire. Make a set of wraps as for a top-drilled bead (Basics, p. 8 and **photo a**). String a 5mm quartz bead onto the wire.

[2] Using chainnose pliers, make a right-angle bend about ⅜ in. (1cm) above the 5mm. Make the first half of a small wrapped loop (Basics).

[3] Hold the loop with pliers, and continue to wrap the stem (**photo b**). Keep the coils close together and uniform, and wrap the entire stem from loop to 5mm crystal. Trim the wire close to the last wrap. Repeat to make a total of eight dangles, varying the length of the wire stem between the 5mm and the wrapped loop slightly with each dangle.

[4] Open one split ring (Basics), and attach four dangles. Repeat with the remaining dangles and another split ring. Add or remove clusters of dangles to earring findings as desired.

Tanzanite clusters

[1] On a head pin, string a 7mm tanzanite bead and a 5mm quartz bead. Make the first half of a wrapped loop (Basics) above the beads, wrapping the stem as in step 3 of "Leaf clusters." Repeat to make a total of eight dangles.

[2] Open a split ring and attach four dangles. Repeat with the remaining four dangles and another split ring. Add or remove clusters of dangles to earring findings as desired.

Pearl clusters

[1] String a pearl onto a head pin, and make the first half of a wrapped loop (Basics).

[2] Cut approximately ½ in. (1.3cm) of chain, and slide an end link into the loop. Finish the wraps (**photo c**).

[3] Repeat steps 1 and 2 13 times, cutting the chain to the desired length for each dangle.

[4] Open a split ring, and attach the top chain link of seven dangles. Repeat with the remaining dangles and another split ring. Make 14 dangles, and divide them evenly between the two split rings. Add or remove clusters of dangles to earring findings as desired.

MATERIALS

all projects
• 2 6mm split rings
• pair of earring findings or hoop earrings, 3mm tubing
• file (optional)
• hammer (optional)
• chainnose pliers
• roundnose pliers
• split-ring pliers
• wire cutters

leaf clusters
• 8 Czech glass leaf beads
• 8 5mm faceted quartz crystal buttons
• 3½ ft. (1m) 24-gauge wire, half hard

tanzanite clusters
• 8 7mm faceted tanzanite buttons
• 8 5mm faceted quartz crystal buttons
• 8 4-in. (10cm) ultra-fine head pins

pearl clusters
• 14 3–5mm pearls
• 14 4-in. (10cm) ultra-fine head pins or 5 ft. (1.4m) 24-gauge wire, half hard
• 12 in. (30cm) chain

Upside down

Free-form wire design — manipulating wire
into abstract shapes — is fun and has limitless
possibilities. Use these earrings as a starting
point for your own designs.

designed by **Charlotte Miller**

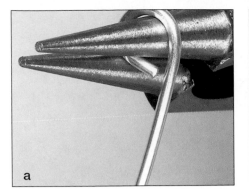

a

b

c

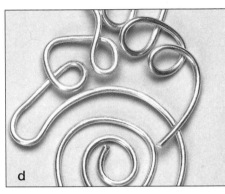

d

e

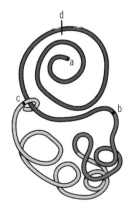

f

step*by*step

[1] Cut two 16-in. (41cm) pieces of wire. If the ends of the wire are sharp, round them with a metal file.

[2] Grasp the end of one of the wires in the middle of the jaws of the roundnose pliers. Bring the wire over one jaw of the pliers to form a simple loop (**photo a**). This is the center loop of the large coil (**figure 1, a**).

[3] Continue forming the coil as illustrated in red in the **figure 1** template. Since the coil is large, you might find it easier to use your fingers to form the coil rather than pliers (**photo b**).

[4] Form the rest of the wire shape using roundnose pliers (**photo c**), following the template from blue to yellow (**figure 1, b–c**).

[5] The end of the wire is now crossing the outer ring of the coil. Trim the wire about ¼ in. (6mm) past the point where it crosses the edge of the coil (**photo d**).

[6] Grasp the end of the wire with roundnose pliers, and make a small hook toward the coil. Slide the outside ring of the coil into the hook (**photo e**). Squeeze the hook closed using chainnose pliers.

Optional: Place the wire on an anvil or bench block, and hammer it to add texture and harden the wire (**photo f**).

[7] Open the loop (Basics, p. 8) on an earring finding, and attach it to the wire shape at **point d** of **figure 1**. Close the loop.

[8] Following the **figure 2** template, repeat steps 2–7 to make a second earring the mirror image of the first.

MATERIALS

one pair earrings

- 32 in. (81cm) 14- or 16-gauge wire, dead soft
- pair of earring findings
- chainnose pliers
- anvil or bench block (optional)
- hammer (optional)
- metal file
- roundnose pliers
- wire cutters

SUPPLY NOTE:

Use either 14- or 16-gauge wire. 16-gauge wire is easier to form since it isn't as thick as 14-gauge. The earrings will also be lighter, so you can add beaded dangles or additional decorative wraps.

FIGURE 1

FIGURE 2

CHAPTER 4
jewelry sets

Enamel sensation

Enhanced by a simple design, fabulous enamel beads show off a glorious array of color. Combine them with crystals in a classic necklace, bracelet, and earring ensemble.

by **Cheryl Phelan**

a

b

c

step*by*step

Necklace

[1] On 8 in. (20cm) of beading cord, pick up a repeating pattern of an 11º seed bead and a 3mm bicone crystal four times. Sew through the hole on the pendant, and pick up a pattern of an 11º and a 3mm crystal four more times.

[2] Tie the tail and working thread together with a square knot (Basics, p. 8) to form the beads into a ring **(photo a)**. Sew through the ring of beads again. Secure the tails with a few half-hitch knots (Basics) between beads, dot the knots with glue, and trim the tails.

[3] Repeat steps 1 and 2 to make a second ring **(photo b)**.

[4] Determine the finished length of your necklace. (This one is 17½ in./ 44.5cm.) Add 6 in. (15cm), and cut a piece of flexible beading wire (Basics) to that length.

[5] Center a 4mm square Czech glass bead, the pendant, a 6mm bicone crystal, and a 4mm square bead on the wire, positioning the crystal between the loops of the pendant **(photo c)**.

[6] On one side of the necklace, string the following pattern: a 5mm bicone crystal, a 5mm enamel bead, a 5mm crystal, a 4mm square bead, a 6mm crystal, a 5mm crystal, a 12mm enamel bead, and a 5mm crystal **(photo d)**. Then string a 6mm crystal, a 4mm crystal, a 6mm crystal, a 5mm crystal, a 12mm enamel bead, a 5mm crystal, and a 6mm crystal **(photo e)**. Repeat on the other side of the necklace.

[7] Continue stringing the patterns from step 6 on both sides of the pendant until your necklace is the desired length minus the length of a clasp.

[8] On one end of the necklace, string a crimp bead, four 11ºs, and the hole on the toggle's ring. Pick up four 11ºs, and go back through the crimp bead and the

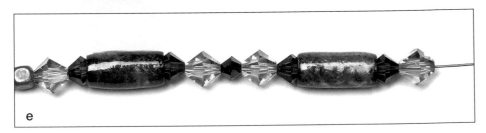

d

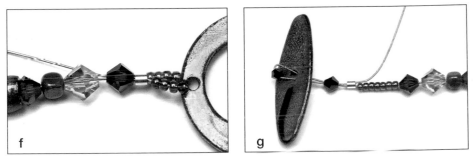

e

f

g

h

next bead or two **(photo f)**. Adjust the wire's tension as needed, crimp the crimp bead (Basics), and trim the tail.

[9] On the other end of the necklace, pick up seven 11ºs, a crimp bead, and a 4mm crystal. Go through the hole on the toggle bar, pick up a 3mm crystal, and go back through the toggle bar, the 4mm crystal, and the crimp bead **(photo g)**. Adjust the tension (see Editor's Note on p. 118), crimp the crimp bead, and trim the tail.

Bracelet

[1] Determine the finished length of your bracelet. Add 5 in. (13cm), and cut a piece of beading wire to that length. Clamp or tape one end.

[2] String a 6mm crystal, a 4mm crystal, a 6mm crystal, a 5mm crystal, a 5mm enamel bead, a 5mm crystal, a 6mm crystal, a 4mm crystal, a 6mm crystal, a 4mm square bead, a 5mm crystal, a 5mm enamel bead, a 5mm crystal, and a 4mm square bead **(photo h)**.

i

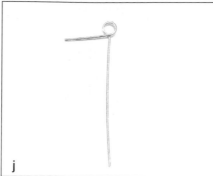

j

k

l

[3] Repeat step 2 until your bracelet is the desired length minus the length of a clasp.
[4] String a crimp bead, go through the loop on one half of the clasp, and go back through the crimp bead and the last two beads strung **(photo i)**.
[5] Adjust the wire's tension, crimp the crimp bead (Basics), and trim the tail.
[6] Remove the clamp or tape and repeat steps 4 and 5 on the other end of the bracelet.

Earrings

[1] Cut a 2-in. (5cm) piece of 22-gauge wire. Make the first half of a wrapped loop (Basics and **photo j**). Slide a domed-circle bead onto the loop, and finish the loop with two wraps (Basics and **photo k**).
[2] Pick up a 6mm bicone crystal, and make a plain loop (Basics) perpendicular to the wrapped loop **(photo l)**.
[3] Open the plain loop (Basics), attach it to the loop on an earring finding, and close the loop.
[4] Make a second earring to match the first.

EDITOR'S NOTE:
Before you crimp the crimp beads on the necklace and bracelet, leave about 4mm of slack in the wire. Without the slack, the 5mm crystals that tuck inside the enamel beads won't be able to flex, leaving your pieces stiff and uncomfortable to wear.

MATERIALS
necklace 17½ in. (44.5cm)
• 38mm domed-circle pendant*
• enamel beads*
  8 12mm regular tubes
  6 5mm shorties
• bicone crystals
  19 6mm, light Colorado topaz champagne
  30 5mm, tourmaline
  5 4mm, jet nut 2x
  17 3mm, jet nut 2x
• 12 4mm square Czech glass beads, lavender
• 1g size 11º Japanese seed beads, dark green
• toggle clasp, enamel*
• 2 crimp beads
• Dandyline beading cord, .006
• flexible beading wire, .012–.014
• beading needles, #12
• G-S Hypo Cement
• crimping pliers
• wire cutters

bracelet 7½ in. (19.1cm)
• 5 5mm enamel beads, shorties*
• bicone crystals
  11 6mm, light Colorado topaz champagne
  10 5mm, tourmaline
  6 4mm, jet nut 2x
• 6 4mm square Czech glass beads, lavender
• toggle clasp
• 2 crimp beads
• flexible beading wire, .012–.014
• clamps or tape
• crimping pliers
• wire cutters

one pair earrings
• 2 15mm domed-circle enamel beads*
• 2 6mm bicone crystals, light Colorado topaz champagne
• 4 in. (10cm) 22-gauge wire, half hard
• pair of earring findings
• chainnose pliers
• roundnose pliers
• wire cutters
* enamel beads and components by Sara Lukkonen of C-Koop Beads, ckoopbeads.com

Charmed
coral set

by **Pam O'Connor**

Combine silver shells, pearls, and coral for the perfect summer set reminiscent of a classic charm bracelet. The seashell charms combine naturally with pearls and coral.

step*by*step

Cone-shaped shell dangles
[1] Cut four five-link pieces of chain (photo a).
[2] On a head pin, string one or two branch coral beads, and make the first half of a wrapped loop (Basics, p. 8). Attach the loop to the end link on one five-link piece of chain, and finish the wraps (photo b). This will be the bottom link of the coral-embellished chain.
[3] Repeat step 2 to add ten more coral dangles to the five-link chain as follows: two more to the bottom link (a total of three dangles) and two dangles to each of the four remaining links.
[4] Cut a 4-in. (10cm) piece of 24-gauge wire. Make the first half of a wrapped loop at one end, attach it to the top link of the embellished chain (photo c), and finish the wraps.

[5] String the cone-shaped shell onto the wire, wide end first (photo d). Make the first half of a wrapped loop above the cone (photo e) and set it aside.
[6] Repeat steps 2–5 with the three remaining five-link chains and cone-shaped shells.

Other shell dangles
[1] String a pearl on a head pin, and make a wrapped loop (photo f). Trim the wire tail. Repeat to make a total of nine pearl dangles.
[2] Cut a 4-in. piece of wire. Make the first half of a wrapped loop, and connect it to the loop on a pearl dangle (photo g). Finish the wrap.
[3] String a shell charm on the wire (photo h). Start a wrapped loop and set the pieces aside.
[4] Repeat steps 2 and 3 with the remaining six shell beads. Hang three

pearl dangles from the wrapped loop below the 20mm center shell bead.

Necklace assembly
[1] Fold the remaining chain (approximately 22 in./56cm) in half to find the center link. Slide the loop above the 20mm shell dangle into the center link of the chain (photo i), and finish the wraps.
[2] Skip three links, and attach a cone-shaped dangle to the next link (photo j).
[3] Skip another three links. Attach a medium shell dangle to the following link (photo k).
[4] Repeat step 3 three times, attaching a cone-shaped dangle and two 10mm shell dangles.
[5] Repeat steps 2–4 on the other side of the necklace.
[6] Check the fit, and shorten the chain the same amount on each side

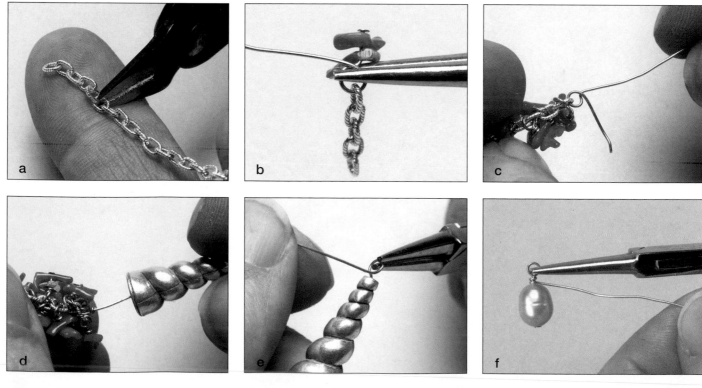

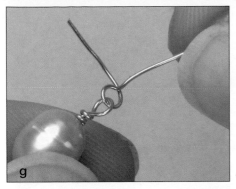

g

h

i

j

k

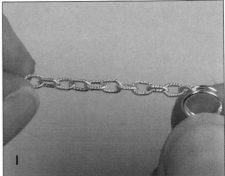

l

as needed, taking into account the length of a clasp.

[7] Attach a split ring to each end link on the chain (photo l). Connect the S-hook clasp between the split rings.

Earrings

[1] Cut two five-link pieces of chain.

[2] Repeat steps 2–5 of "Cone-shaped shell dangles" with one of the chains. Finish the wraps.

[3] Open the loop (Basics) of an earring finding. Attach the dangle, and close the loop.

[4] Repeat steps 2 and 3 to make a second earring to match the first.

MATERIALS

both projects
- chainnose pliers
- roundnose pliers
- split-ring pliers
- wire cutters

necklace 23 in. (58cm)
- silver shell beads
  4 20 x 8mm cone-shaped
  20mm spiral-shaped
  2 18mm clam shell-shaped
  4 10mm clam shell-shaped
- 9 5 x 7mm pearls
- 44–88 branch coral beads
- S-hook clasp
- 4 ft. (1.3m) 24-gauge sterling silver wire, half hard
- 26 in. (66cm) chain, 2–3mm links
- 53 2-in. (5cm) ultra-thin head pins
- 2 5mm split rings

one pair earrings
- 2 20 x 8mm cone-shaped shell beads
- 22–44 branch coral beads
- 8 in. (20cm) 24-gauge wire
- 2 in. (5cm) chain, 2–3mm links
- pair of earring findings

Faux
lariat

Lariats are great, except when they start to feel like a noose! With this design, you don't have to actually wrap these lovely strands around your neck — you just knot two long, slinky strands of beads.

by **Pam O'Connor**

step*by*step

Necklace

[1] Measure your neckline, and subtract the length of a clasp. Add 5 in. (13cm), and cut a piece of flexible beading wire (Basics, p. 8) to that length.
[2] Clamp or tape one end of the beading wire. String an alternating pattern of 8º seed beads and 9 x 6mm faceted stone beads to the desired length.
[3] String a crimp bead and a loop on one half of a clasp. Go back through the crimp and the next few beads. Tighten the loop, crimp the crimp bead (Basics and **photo a**), and trim the tail.
[4] Remove the clamp or tape from the other end, snug up the beads, and repeat step 3.
[5] Cut a 25-in. (64cm) piece of flexible beading wire. String an 8º and a crimp 2 in. (5cm) from the wire's end. Feed the wire end back through the crimp, and crimp it (**photo b**).

[6] String a flower bead, an 8º, a flower bead, an 8º, and a flower bead over the wire and the wire tail (**photo c**).
[7] String an alternating pattern of an 8º and a stone bead until the beaded strand measures approximately 20 in. (51cm). String a crimp bead.
[8] Repeat step 3 to attach the beaded strand to a remaining loop on one side of the clasp.
[9] Repeat steps 5–8 to make the other lariat strand. Knot the strands together with an overhand knot (Basics).

Earrings

[1] On a head pin, string an 8º, a flower bead, an 8º, a flower bead, an 8º, a stone bead, and an 8º, and make a wrapped loop (Basics).
[2] Open the loop (Basics) of an earring finding and attach the wrapped loop. Close the loop.
[3] Make a second earring to match the first.

MATERIALS
necklace 20 in. (51cm)
- 6 20 x 10mm glass flower beads
- 3 16-in. (41cm) strands 9 x 6mm faceted stone beads
- 7g size 8º seed beads
- 2-strand clasp
- 6 crimp beads
- flexible beading wire, .014
- clamps or tape
- crimping pliers
- wire cutters

one pair earrings
- 4 20 x 10mm glass flower beads
- 2 9 x 6mm faceted stone beads
- 8 size 8º seed beads
- 2 3-in. (7.6cm) head pins
- pair of earring findings
- chainnose pliers
- roundnose pliers
- wire cutters

a

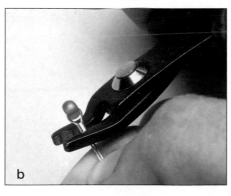
b

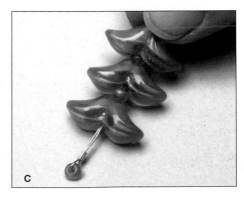
c

Silver cascade

Simply strung, this necklace can be casual or dramatic, depending on the length and quantity of strands. Make one with strands of all the same length to support a pendant. String short strands for a coordinating bracelet.

designed by **Glenda Payseno**

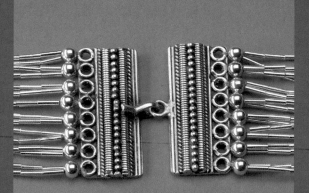

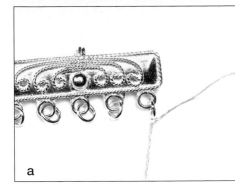

a

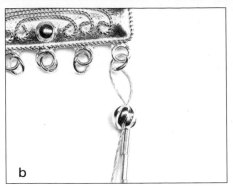

b

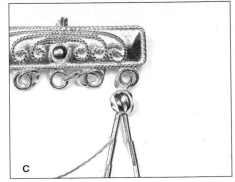

c

step*by*step

Necklace

[1] Measure your neckline to determine the length of the shortest strand. The shortest strand of this necklace is 16 in. (41cm).

[2] Condition a 1½-yd. (1.4m) piece of beading thread (Basics, p. 8), and leaving a 4-in. (10cm) tail, tie the end of the thread to the first loop on a clasp with a surgeon's knot (Basics and **photo a**).

[3] Pick up a 4mm bead, 70 liquid silver beads, and a 4mm bead. To start with a different length, adjust the number of liquid silver beads until the strand fits comfortably around your neck. Sew through the corresponding loop on the other half of the clasp.

[4] Sew back through the 4mm bead **(photo b)**. Pull the beads snug against the clasp. Pick up 75 liquid silver beads (or five more than the previous strand), and sew through the 4mm bead and the first clasp loop on the other side of the necklace.

[5] Tie the working thread and the tail together with a surgeon's knot (Basics). To complete the first pair of strands, thread a needle on a tail, and pull it into the 4mm bead and the first few liquid silver beads. Dot the knot with glue if desired, pull so the knot slips into the 4mm bead **(photo c)**, and trim. Repeat with the other tail.

[6] Repeat steps 1–4 to string two strands from each clasp loop. Increase the length of thread by 5 in. (13cm) for each new pair of strands. Increase the liquid silver beads by five for every strand.

Bracelet

Work the bracelet in the same manner as the necklace, but make all the strands the same length. You can also add more strands to each loop of the clasp to make a more substantial bracelet.

EDITOR'S NOTE:

If the 4mm beads have large holes, the liquid silver beads may slip into them, making the necklace more difficult to string. You can avoid this by using beads with smaller holes or by stringing a 2mm silver bead or 11° seed bead between the liquid silver beads and the 4mm beads.

MATERIALS

both projects
- conditioned beading thread, size D, or Fireline 6 lb. test
- beading needles, #12 sharps
- G-S Hypo Cement (optional)

necklace 23 in. (58cm)
- 1½ oz. 6mm liquid silver bugle beads
- 8–16 4mm silver beads
- 4–8-strand silver clasp

bracelet 7 in. (18cm)
- ½ oz. 6mm liquid silver bugle beads
- 8 4mm silver beads
- 4-strand silver slide clasp

Tears of joy

String small teardrop beads between large
glass beads for an easy, yet substantial,
two-strand necklace. The matching bracelet
and earrings are a cinch.

designed by **Helene Tsigistras**

a

b

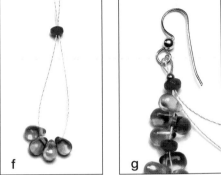

c

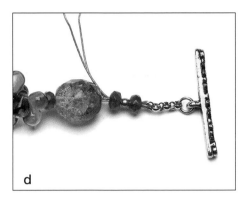

d

e

f

g

step*by*step

Necklace

[1] Cut a 4-ft. (1.2m) piece of beading wire (Basics, p. 8), and center the loop of one half of a clasp.

[2] Over both ends, string a rondelle and a crimp bead **(photo a)**. Crimp the crimp bead (Basics).

[3] Over both ends, string a rondelle, a 10mm bead, and a rondelle **(photo b)**.

[4] Separate the wires, and string ten teardrop beads on each wire **(photo c)**.

[5] Repeat steps 3 and 4 nine times. Repeat step 3. You should use 11 10mm beads.

[6] Over both ends, string a crimp bead, a rondelle, and the other half of the clasp. Go back through the last three beads **(photo d)**. Snug up the beads to remove any slack. Crimp the crimp bead, and trim the wire ends.

Bracelet

[1] Cut a 20-in. (51cm) piece of beading wire (Basics), and center the loop of one half of a clasp. Follow steps 2 and 3 of the necklace.

[2] Follow step 4 of the necklace, but string six teardrop beads on each end instead of ten **(photo e)**.

[3] Repeat the pattern (rondelle, 10mm, rondelle alternating with six teardrops) four times. You should use five 10mm beads and will end with teardrops.

[4] Over both ends, string a rondelle, then finish as in step 6 of the necklace.

Earrings

[1] Cut a 6-in. (15cm) piece of beading wire, and center four teardrop beads on it. String a rondelle over both ends **(photo f)**.

[2] String two teardrops on each end. Over both ends, string a rondelle, a crimp bead, and an earring wire. Go back through the crimp bead and the top rondelle **(photo g)**. Snug up the beads, and crimp the crimp bead (Basics). Trim the excess wire.

[3] Make a second earring to match the first.

MATERIALS

all projects
- flexible beading wire, .014
- crimping pliers
- wire cutters

necklace 20 in. (51cm)
- 11 10mm round or faceted glass beads
- 200 4 x 6mm teardrop beads
- 24 4 x 6mm rondelles
- toggle clasp
- 2 crimp beads

bracelet 7 in. (18cm)
- 5 10mm round or faceted glass beads
- 60 4 x 6mm teardrop beads
- 13 4 x 6mm rondelles
- toggle clasp
- 2 crimp beads

one pair earrings
- 16 4 x 6mm teardrop beads
- 4 4 x 6mm rondelles
- 2 crimp beads
- pair of earring wires

Pearls just want to have fun

Crystal pearls dance and swing on this bracelet with matching earrings. Add a variation on wrapped loops for an alternative to the traditional charm bracelet.

designed by **Maryann Scandiffio-Humes**

EDITOR'S NOTE:
The wrapped loops used in these projects are larger than standard wrapped loops and should have little or no stem at the base. This allows you to begin the wraps right on top of the bead, producing a spiraling cap. Be sure to get comfortable with the technique using craft or copper wire before beginning either project.

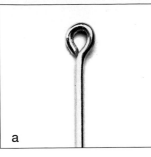

a

b

c

d

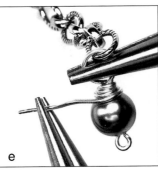

e

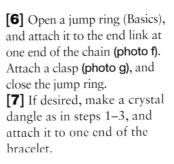

f

g

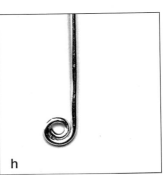

h

i

j

MATERIALS

both projects

- chainnose pliers
- roundnose pliers
- wire cutters

bracelet 7¼ in. (19.1cm)

- 15 8mm round crystal pearls in a mix of 3 colors
- 22 6mm round crystal pearls in a mix of 5 colors
- 4mm bicone crystal (optional)
- clasp
- 8 ft. (2.4m) 22-gauge wire, half hard
- 7¼ in. (18.4cm) cable chain, 6mm links
- 4–5mm jump ring

one pair earrings

- 2 8mm round crystal pearls
- 2 5–6mm bicone crystals
- 6 in. (15cm) 22-gauge wire, half hard
- pair of earring findings

step*by*step

Bracelet

[1] Cut a 2½-in. (6.4cm) piece of wire, and make a plain loop (Basics, p. 8, and **photo a**) at one end.

[2] String a pearl, and bend the wire at a right angle (**photo b**).

[3] Using the wide part of the roundnose pliers, make the first half of a large wrapped loop (Basics) right above the bead (**photo c**). Repeat, making a total of 37 pearl dangles.

[4] Slide the loop of a pearl dangle into the end chain link (**photo d**). Repeat with the remaining pearls, distributing the colors and sizes evenly along the length and on both sides of the chain.

[5] When you're pleased with the placement of the pearls, grasp the wire tail on a dangle, and wrap it around the base of the loop. Continue wrapping two or three times around the top of the pearl, forming a spiral cap (**photo e**). Trim the excess wire.

Repeat with the remaining pearl dangles.

[6] Open a jump ring (Basics), and attach it to the end link at one end of the chain (**photo f**). Attach a clasp (**photo g**), and close the jump ring.

[7] If desired, make a crystal dangle as in steps 1–3, and attach it to one end of the bracelet.

Earrings

[1] Cut a 3-in. (7.6cm) piece of wire, and make a small coil at one end (**photo h**). String a crystal and a pearl, and press the coil up against the crystal (**photo i**).

[2] Make the first half of a large wrapped loop above the bead, as in steps 2 and 3 of the bracelet.

[3] Slide the dangle through the loop on an earring finding (**photo j**), and finish the spiraling wraps, as in step 5 of the bracelet. Trim the excess wire.

[4] Make a second earring to match the first.

Focus on findings

Combine gemstones, crystals, and pearls to showcase textured silver components in simple but elegant jewelry.

designed by **Juana Jelen**

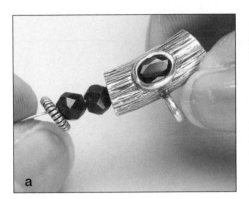

a

b

step*by*step

Necklace with tube bead

[1] Cut a 20-in. (51cm) piece of flexible beading wire (Basics, p. 8), and center the tube bead on it.

[2] On one side, string a repeating pattern of 6mm stone rondelles and 2–5mm silver spacers until you reach half the desired length minus the length of a clasp. If the beads are smaller than the hole of the tube bead, fill the tube with beads so it hangs nicely, and string a spacer bead on each side of the tube to keep the tube from sliding over the beads **(photo a)**. Repeat on the other side of the necklace.

[3] On one end, string a crimp bead, a stone or silver bead, and the loop on one half of a clasp. Go back through the bead, crimp, and another bead or two. If the stones have small holes and the wire won't go back through a second time, string a 3mm round silver spacer on each side of the crimp bead (see the peridot necklace with a centerpiece component on p. 130 at right). Crimp the crimp bead (Basics), and trim the excess wire.

[4] Snug up the beads, and repeat on the other end of the necklace.

[5] To add a dangle to the tube bead, string a large stone and a silver spacer on a head pin. Make the first half of a wrapped loop (Basics), and slide it through the loop on the tube bead. Finish the wraps.

[6] To add a dangle at the end of the necklace, string a stone rondelle and a silver spacer on a head pin, and make the first half of a wrapped loop. Slide the loop onto a loop on the clasp, and finish the wraps.

Necklace with centerpiece component

[1] Cut a 2-in. (5cm) piece of 22-gauge wire. Make a plain loop (Basics) at one end. String a silver spacer, and slide the wire through the hole on the bottom of the square component. String enough seed beads to fill the inside of the component, and pass the wire through the hole on the top of the component.

[2] Make a bend in the wire perpendicular to the loop **(photo b)**. Trim the wire to ³⁄₈ in. (1cm), and make a plain loop.

[3] Repeat steps 1 and 2 twice. String two spacers after the loop on the middle wire **(photo c)**.

[4] Cut a 20-in. (51cm) piece of flexible beading wire (Basics), and string the

MATERIALS

all projects
- clasp
- chainnose pliers
- crimping pliers
- roundnose pliers
- wire cutters

necklace with tube bead (p. 130, left) 16 in. (41cm)
- tube bead*
- 15mm faceted stone bead (for dangle)
- 16 in. (41cm) strand 6mm faceted stone rondelles
- 15 2–5mm silver spacer beads
- 3 in. (7.6cm) 22-gauge wire, half hard (optional)
- 2 2-in. (5cm) head pins
- 2 crimp beads
- flexible beading wire, .012–.014

necklace with centerpiece component (p. 130, right) 17 in. (43cm)
- square centerpiece component*
- 16-in. (41cm) strand 4mm faceted stone or glass beads
- 30–35 2–8mm silver beads and spacers
- 6 in. (15cm) 22-gauge wire, half hard
- 4 2-in. (5cm) head pins
- flexible beading wire, .012–.014

bracelet (p. 130, center) 7 in. (18cm)
- square centerpiece component*
- 2 6–8mm round silver beads
- 24 6mm silver tube beads
- 44 4mm pearls
- 30 4mm bicone crystals
- 1g seed beads, size 8º (optional)
- 2 3mm round silver spacers
- 3–5 head pins (optional)
- 2 crimp beads
- flexible beading wire, .010

* Pacific Silverworks, pacificsilverworks.com

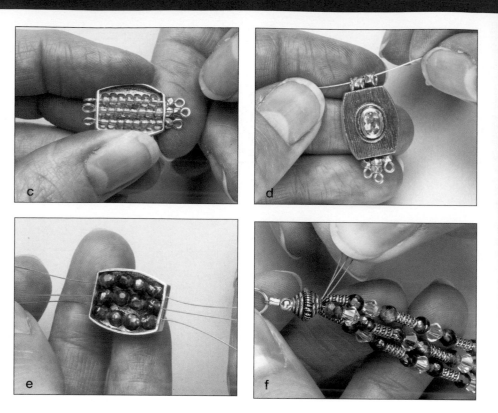

first loop above the square component. String a 3mm bead, the next loop, a 3mm bead, and the third loop (photo d). Center the component on the beading wire.

[5] String a repeating pattern of stone and silver beads on each side of the necklace for the desired length.

[6] Follow steps 3 and 4 of "Necklace with tube bead" to finish the ends.

[7] To make the centerpiece dangles, string a combination of stone and silver beads on a head pin, and make a plain loop. Open the loop, and attach it to an end loop under the component. Repeat twice to make the middle dangle, but make it longer and attach it to the middle loop. Repeat to make a third dangle that matches the first, attaching it to the remaining end loop.

[8] Make another dangle, and attach it to the jump ring on the clasp.

Bracelet

[1] Cut three 12-in. (30cm) pieces of flexible beading wire (Basics).

[2] Pass the end of one wire through a hole on the component. String enough pearls or 8° seed beads to span the inside of the component, and pass the wire through the hole on the other end of the component. Repeat with the remaining strands (photo e).

[3] Center the component on the three wires and string a repeating pattern of pearls, crystals, silver beads on each wire on both sides of the component. Adjust the pattern for each strand so the same beads don't line up next to each other.

[4] Pass all three wires through a silver bead and a crimp. If the silver bead's hole slides over the crimp, string a 3mm round bead between the bead and the crimp. Go through a loop on a clasp and back through the crimp and silver beads (photo f). Crimp the crimp bead (Basics) and trim the wires. Repeat at the other end.

[5] Follow step 6 of "Necklace with tube bead" to attach four crystal dangles to the jump ring on the clasp.

Chandelier ensemble

Make a delicate necklace-and-earring ensemble with tiers of wire arches. Accented with small, faceted dangles, this set is light as a feather and oh, so wearable.

by **Julia Gerlach**

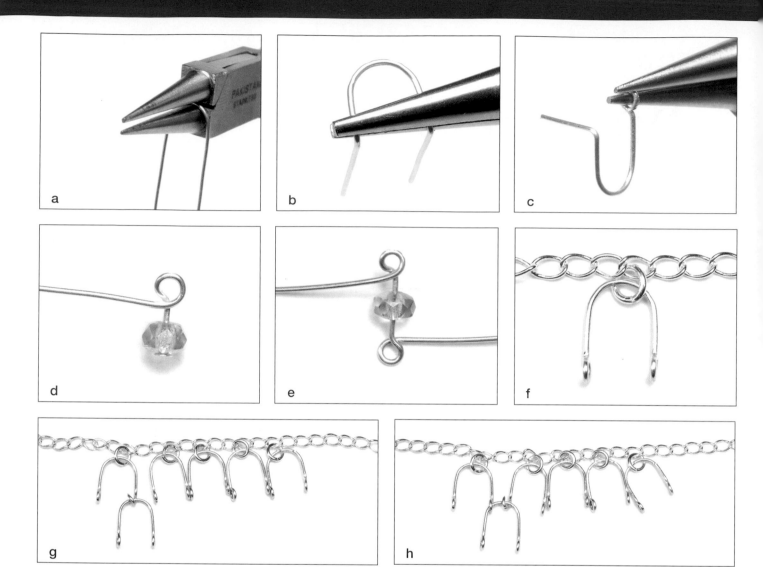

step*by*step

Necklace components

[1] Cut 15 1½-in. (3.8cm) pieces of 22-gauge wire.

[2] Curve a piece of wire around the widest part of one jaw of your round-nose pliers, forming an arch (**photo a**).

[3] Using your chainnose pliers, bend each wire end into a right angle ⁵⁄₁₆ in. (8mm) from the curve (**photo b**).

[4] Trim the wire ends to ⁵⁄₁₆ in., and make a small plain loop (Basics, p. 8 and **photo c**) on each.

[5] Repeat steps 2–4 with the remaining 14 wires.

[6] On a head pin, string a 3 x 5mm rondelle, and make the first half of a wrapped loop (Basics and **photo d**). Repeat with the remaining 24 head pins.

[7] Cut a 2½-in. (6.4cm) piece of wire, and make the first half of a wrapped loop on one end. String a rondelle, and

make the first half of a wrapped loop on the other end (**photo e**). Make a total of six wrapped-loop units.

[8] Cut six 1¾-in. (4.4cm) pieces of chain.

Necklace assembly

[1] Cut a 3¾-in. (9.5cm) piece of chain with an odd number of links.

[2] Open a 4mm jump ring (Basics), and slide it through the center chain link. Attach a wire arch, and close the jump ring (**photo f**).

[3] On each side of the first arch, skip two or three links, and repeat step 2 with another wire arch, making sure that the loops at the base of the arches all face the same way. Repeat. Make any necessary adjustments so the five arches hang side by side without overlapping or leaving gaps.

[4] Open the inner loop of an end arch, and attach the curved part of an arch (**photo g**). Close the loop. Open the loop

of the adjacent arch, and attach it to the same arch (**photo h**). Close the loop.

[5] Continue connecting arches in this manner until you have five rows. There should be five arches in the first row, four in the second, three in the third, two in the fourth, and one in the final row (**photo i**).

[6] Attach the loop of a rondelle dangle to two adjacent arch loops. Finish the wraps (**photo j**). Repeat to attach a rondelle dangle to each single loop and pair of loops. Also attach one rondelle dangle to each jump ring that connects the pendant to the chain.

[7] Attach one loop of a wrapped-loop unit to the end chain link (**photo k**). Finish the wraps.

[8] Attach an end link of a 1¾-in. piece of chain to the other wrapped loop, and finish the wraps (**photo l**).

[9] Repeat steps 7 and 8 twice.

[10] Repeat steps 7–9 on the other end.

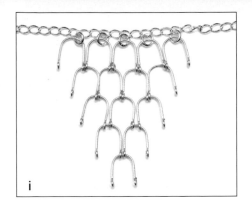

i

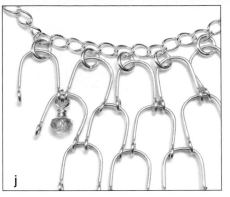

j

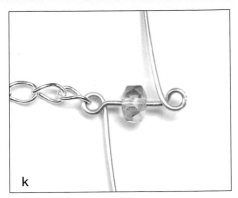

k

l

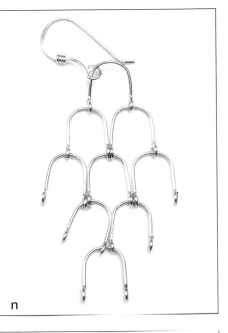

m

n

[11] Open a jump ring, and connect the end chain link to one half of a clasp **(photo m)**. Close the loop. Repeat on the other end.

Earrings

[1] Make 18 wire arches as in steps 1–4 of "Necklace components."

[2] Make 28 rondelle dangles as in step 6 of "Necklace components."

[3] Open the loop (Basics) of an earring finding, and attach it to one wire arch. Close the loop.

[4] Connect the wire arches so you have five rows: one arch in the first row, two in the second, three in the third, two in the fourth, and one in the final row **(photo n)**.

[5] Attach the rondelle dangles as in step 6 of "Necklace assembly."

[6] Repeat steps 3–5 to make a second earring.

EDITOR'S NOTE:
When you're not wearing these pieces, hang them up to prevent tangling.

MATERIALS
both projects
- chainnose pliers
- roundnose pliers
- wire cutters

necklace 18 in. (46cm)
- 31 3 x 5mm faceted glass rondelles
- clasp
- 4 ft. (1.2m) 22-gauge wire, half hard
- 18 in. (46cm) curb chain, 2–3mm links
- 25 1½-in. (3.8cm) head pins
- 7 4mm jump rings

one pair earrings
- 28 3 x 5mm faceted glass rondelles
- 3 ft. (.9m) 22-gauge wire, half hard
- 28 1½-in. (3.8cm) head pins
- pair of earring findings

Garland necklace

String a strand of easy-to-make components to create the illusion of an intricate necklace.

designed by **Sharon Lester**

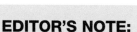

a

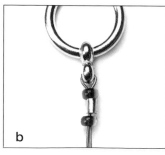

b

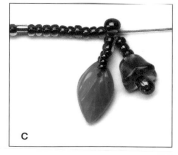

c

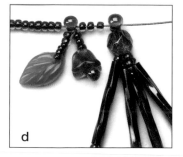

d

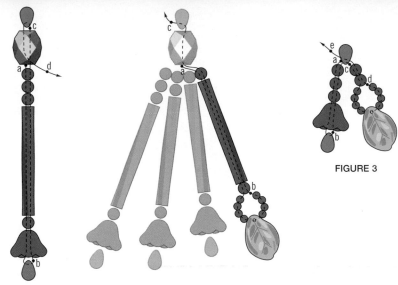

FIGURE 1   FIGURE 2

FIGURE 3

MATERIALS
both projects
- conditioned beading thread, color to match beads
- beading needles, #12
- G-S Hypo Cement

necklace 15 in. (38cm)
- 92 10mm twisted bugle beads
- 47 10mm leaves, drilled front to back
- 93 6mm flowers
- 23 6mm round glass beads
- 140 3mm drop beads
- seed beads
  20g size 11º
  10g size 15º
- toggle clasp
- 2 crimp beads
- flexible beading wire, .014
- crimping pliers
- wire cutters

earrings
- 8 10mm twisted bugle beads
- 2 10mm leaves, drilled front to back
- 2 6mm round glass beads
- 6 6mm flowers
- 8 drop beads
- seed beads
  22 size 11º
  16 size 15º
- pair of ball-post earring findings with loop

step*by*step

Large cluster
[1] Thread a needle with a comfortable length of conditioned beading thread (Basics, p. 8). Pick up a drop bead, and leaving a 3-in. (7.6cm) tail, tie the working thread and tail with a square knot (Basics) above the drop.
[2] Pick up a 6mm round bead, and slide it next to the drop, covering both threads (photo a). Trim the tail just beyond the 6mm.
[3] Pick up three 11º seed beads, a bugle bead, an 11º, a flower bead, and a drop bead (figure 1, a–b).
[4] Skip the drop, and go back through all the beads, exiting the top of the 6mm (b–c). Sew through the first drop again, and continue back through the 6mm (c–d).
[5] Repeat steps 3 and 4, but start with two 11ºs.
[6] Repeat steps 3 and 4, but start with one 11º.
[7] Pick up one 11º, a bugle, an 11º, four 15º seed beads, a leaf bead, and four 15ºs (figure 2, a–b).

[8] Sew back through the 11º, bugle, and 11º, and continue through the 6mm and the drop (b–c). Tie several half-hitch knots (Basics) around the main thread between the drop and the 6mm bead. Dot the knots with glue and let them dry. Exit the 6mm bead and trim the tail.
[9] Repeat steps 1–8 to make a total of 24 large clusters.

Small cluster
[1] Repeat step 1 of "Large cluster." Pick up three 11ºs, a flower, and a drop (figure 3, a–b). Skip the drop, and sew back through the flower, the three 11ºs, and the top drop (b–c).
[2] Pick up two 11ºs, four 15ºs, a leaf, and four 15ºs (c–d). Sew back through the two 11ºs and the drop (d–e). Tie several half-hitch knots, and dot them with glue. Sew through several beads, and trim the tail.
[3] Repeat steps 1 and 2 to make a total of 23 small clusters.

Necklace assembly
[1] Cut a piece of flexible beading wire (Basics) 6 in. (15cm) longer than the desired finished length. String an 11º, a crimp bead, an 11º, and the loop on one half of a toggle clasp. Go back through the 11º and the crimp bead. Crimp the crimp bead (Basics and photo b), and trim the tail.
[2] String nine 11ºs and the top drop of a small cluster (photo c).
[3] String three 11ºs and a large cluster (photo d). Alternate between small and

large clusters, separating them with groups of three 11ºs, until all the clusters are strung. End with a small cluster.
[4] String nine 11ºs, a crimp bead, and an 11º, and the loop on the other end of the toggle clasp. Go back through the 11º and the crimp bead.
[5] Tighten the wire, and crimp the crimp bead. Go back through several more seed beads, and trim the excess wire.

Earrings
[1] Tie the end of a 2-ft. (61cm) length of conditioned beading thread (Basics) to the loop on the earring finding with an overhand knot (Basics).
[2] Make a large cluster as for the necklace, but omit the drop and start with the 6mm (photo e).
[3] Make a second earring to match the first.

Delicate drops

Sparkling teardrop crystals add character to a basic chain necklace and earrings. The necklace is simple enough for everyday wear, so you'll find yourself reaching for it often.

designed by **Helene Tsigistras**

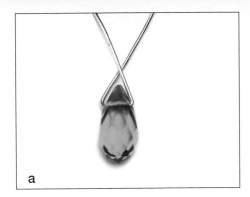

a

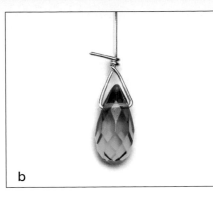

b

c

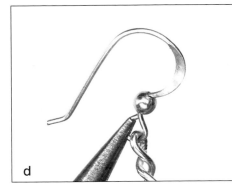

d

e

f

stepbystep

Necklace

[1] Make a 45-degree bend ¾ in. (1.9cm) from the end of the wire with your chainnose pliers. Slide a crystal next to the bend, and make another 45-degree bend on the other side of the crystal **(photo a)**. Make two wraps above the crystal with the wire remaining from the first bend **(photo b)**. Trim the excess wire. Cut the long wire 1½ in. (3.8cm) above the wraps. Repeat to make a total of eight dangles.

[2] Make the first half of a wrapped loop (Basics, p. 8) above the wraps on one of the dangles.

[3] Repeat step 2 with the remaining dangles.

[4] Attach the loop to the twelfth large link from one end of the chain. Finish the wraps **(photo c)**. Trim the excess wire.

[5] Skip a large link, and attach a dangle to the next large link. Finish the wraps.

[6] Repeat step 5 with the remaining dangles.

[7] Open a jump ring (Basics), and connect the last link of the chain to one half of a clasp. Repeat on the other end with the other half of the clasp.

Earrings

[1] Cut two pieces of chain with three figure-8 links and three large links each.

[2] Open the loop (Basics) of an earring finding, and attach the end figure-8 link of one piece **(photo d)**.

[3] Make three dangles as in step 1 of the necklace. Attach the first dangle to the bottom half of the second figure-8 link with a wrapped loop. Repeat with the other two dangles, attaching one to the second large link and one to the third large link **(photo e)**.

[4] On a head pin, string a 4mm bicone crystal, and make the first half of a wrapped loop. Attach the loop to the top half of the second figure-8 link, and finish the wraps. Repeat with a second 4mm, and attach it to the top half of the third figure-8 link **(photo f)**.

[5] Make a second earring to match the first.

MATERIALS

both projects
- chainnose pliers
- roundnose pliers
- wire cutters

necklace 19 in. (48cm)
- 8 5 x 10mm crystal briolettes
- toggle clasp
- 25 in. (64cm) 22-gauge wire
- 18 in. (46cm) figure-8 chain, 5mm links
- 2 jump rings

one pair earrings
- 6 5 x 10mm crystal briolettes
- 4 4mm bicone crystals
- 18 in. (46cm) 22-gauge wire
- 2½ in. (6.4cm) figure-8 chain, 5mm links
- 4 24-gauge head pins
- pair of earring findings

Triple-take garnets

Float slivers of silver between garnet beads for a classic three-strand necklace. Simple drop earrings complete this sophisticated ensemble.

designed by **Helene Tsigistras**

a

b

c

d

step*by*step

Necklace

[1] Determine the length of the shortest strand of your necklace. (The shortest strand of this necklace is 15 in./38cm.) Add 6 in. (15cm), and cut a piece of beading wire to that length (Basics, p. 8). Cut a second piece 2 in. (5cm) longer than the first, and cut a third piece 2 in. longer than the second.

[2] On the shortest wire, center a silver tube bead. On each end, string a 4mm bead, a 5mm bead, five 6mm beads, and six 5mms. String 4mms until the strand is 1 in. (2.5cm) short of the desired length. On each end, string a crimp bead and a 4mm. Clamp or tape the ends (photo a).

[3] On the medium wire, center a silver tube bead. On each end, string a 4mm, a 5mm, seven 6mms, 17 5mms, and enough 4mms to yield a strand that is 1 in. longer than the first strand. On each end, string a crimp bead and a 4mm. Clamp or tape the ends.

[4] On the longest wire, center the last silver tube bead. On each end, string a 4mm, a 5mm, 19 6mms, 15 5mms, and enough 4mms to yield a strand that is 1 in. longer than the second strand.

On each end, string a crimp bead and a 4mm. Clamp or tape the ends.

[5] Unclamp or untape one end of the medium strand, and attach the middle loop of a clasp. Go back through the last 4mm, the crimp bead, and the next two beads (photo b). Repeat on the other end.

[6] Repeat step 5 with the other two strands, going through the corresponding loops. Test the fit, and add or remove beads if necessary.

[7] Crimp the crimp beads (Basics), and trim the excess wire.

Earrings

[1] On 6 in. (15cm) of beading wire, string a silver tube bead, a 6mm bead, and a tube bead.

[2] String a crimp bead over both ends (photo c).

[3] String the ends through the loop of an earring finding and back through the crimp bead (photo d). Snug up the wires, and crimp the crimp bead (Basics). Trim the tails.

[4] Make a second earring to match the first.

EDITOR'S NOTE:

The hole sizes in natural gemstone beads vary widely. Be certain that the last few beads at the end of each necklace strand will accommodate two passes with the beading wire so you can attach the clasp.

MATERIALS

both projects
• flexible beading wire, .012
• crimping pliers
• wire cutters

necklace 15–17 in. (38–43cm)
• 3 26 x 2mm sterling silver curved tube beads
• 3 16-in. (41cm) strands of round garnet beads, 1 in each of 3 sizes: 6mm, 5mm, 4mm
• 3-strand clasp
• 6 crimp beads
• clamps or tape

one pair earrings
• 4 26 x 1mm sterling silver curved tube beads
• 2 6mm round garnet beads
• 2 crimp beads
• pair of earring findings

Contributors

Contact **Janice Berkebile** via e-mail at janice@wiredarts.net, or visit her Web site, wiredarts.net.

May Brisebois is the owner of a bead store in Cumming, Ga. Contact her at BEADiful, 678-455-7858, or visit her Web site at maybdesigns.com.

Mindy Brooks is the founding editor of *BeadStyle* magazine and a former editor of *Bead&Button*. Contact her in care of Kalmbach Books.

Contact **Kelly Charveaux** at Scottsdale Bead Supply, 480-945-5988, or via e-mail at scottsdalebeadsupply@msn.com.

Contact **Annie Corkill** via e-mail at andraneal@verizon.net.

Miachelle DePiano is a technical writer as well as a jewelry designer in Gilbert, Ariz. Contact Miachelle at 480-242-9094, via e-mail at cosmoaccessories@cox.net, or visit her Web site, cosmopolitanaccessories.net.

Anna Elizabeth Draeger is Associate Editor at *Bead&Button*. Contact her at adraeger@beadandbutton.com.

Gloria Farver is a frequent contributor to *Bead&Button* magazine. Contact her via e-mail at rfarver@wi.rr.com.

Dale Feuer is a jewelry artist in Bethesda, Md., who draws inspiration from the endless possibilities of designing with seed beads. Contact her via e-mail at dlfeuer@cs.com, or via her Web site, palefiredesigns.net.

Contact **Erika Frost** via e-mail at erikaeliz@hotmail.com.

Julia Gerlach is Managing Editor at *Bead&Button*. Contact her at jgerlach@beadandbutton.com.

Linda Hartung is an avid jewelry designer and teacher whose designs and techniques are featured in many beading and jewelry-making publications around the world. Contact her via e-mail at linda@alacarteclasps.com, or visit her Web sites, alacarteclasps.com or wirelace.com.

Contact **Juana Jelen** via e-mail at sales@pacificsilverworks.com.

Contact **Zurina Ketola** via e-mail at zurina@zurinaketola.com, or visit her Web site, zurinaketola.com.

Alice Korach is the founding editor of *Bead&Button* magazine and author of *Designing with Cubes and Triangles* and *Designing with Cubes and Triangles 2*. Her artwork is displayed at lostwaxglass.com. Contact her via e-mail at akorach@gmail.com.

Sarah Ladiges is an owner of the Bead Hut, in Kirkland, Wash. Contact her at 425-827-6286.

Contact **Sharon Lester** via e-mail at mamalester@yahoo.com.

Melody MacDuffee is a fiber, wire, and bead artist who lives and works in Mobile, Ala. Contact her via e-mail at writersink@msn.com.

Contact **Louise Malcolm** in care of Kalmbach Books.

Irina Miech is an artist, teacher, and the author of a series of popular how-to books on metal clay jewelry design for beaders. She also oversees Eclectica, a retail bead business and classroom studio, where she teaches classes in beading, wirework, and metal clay. Her books include *Metal Clay for Beaders*, *More Metal Clay for Beaders*, *Inventive Metal Clay*, and *Beautiful Wire Jewelry for Beaders*. Contact her via e-mail at eclecticainfo@sbcglobal.net, or visit her Web site at eclecticabeads.com.

Charlotte R. Miller sculpts sterling silver wire into abstract and figurative shapes, stringing them with beads to create wearable jewelry or tabletop tableaux. Contact her via e-mail at crmartist@aol.com.

Contact **Debbie Nishihara** in care of Kalmbach Books.